To Trup,

Attack Life
On All Fronts

by

A. E. Gix

Grosvenor House
Publishing Limited

http://www.attacklifeonallfronts.com

First published in April 2010 by
Piotr Slawomir Kucharski www.anvomir.com

This book is published by
Grosvenor House Publishing Ltd
28-30 High Street, Guildford, Surrey, GU1 3HY.
www.grosvenorhousepublishing.co.uk

A CIP record for this book
is available from the British Library

ISBN 978-1-907652-10-3

For my little Boo,

My awesomeness only has meaning because of You.

Contents

Introduction

Danger! New Ideas, Radical Paradigm Changes and Far-out, Hippie-ish Metaphysical Beliefs Ahead!

If you are a closed-minded person, I suggest you sell this book to one of your open-minded friends. Please note that I'm assuming you have friends, let alone open-minded ones. That's the end of my initial shock treatment; if you're still reading please believe that I'm actually aspiring to be a nice and loving person.

Now that I've discouraged Mr. or Mrs. Fears-Change from reading on, let us begin delving deep into the roots of everything we experience in life. Everything that happens to us of which we are consciously aware, and some things of which we are not.

'Everything?! This book doesn't look thick enough to cover everything that happens in my life, this guy's off his face', you might be saying to yourself.

If you're thinking that, then you're only half right, about me being slightly intoxicated that is. No, but seriously, I am going to attempt to touch on all the aspects of life that I consider a priority. I will attempt to bring into focus the important areas so that all the little things in between will fall into place naturally.

The truth is, all of our reality and reasons why things happen the way they do aren't all that complicated. There are conventional scientists, mathematicians, and quantum physicists all arguing about the mysteries of life and worrying about 'the latest theory'; when the most important question should always be: 'what should *I* believe, that will make me happiest?' One does not need to know all the intricacies and details of a particular technology or ideology to enjoy its benefits. For example, if one was just accept that matter and energy are interchangeable and that all this 'energy/magnetism/bio field/vibration/attraction mumbo jumbo' is actually fact; then the ramifications and applications of personal interpretations of these facts will no doubt bring about at least some benefit in some way.

Does it really matter *how* it works, as long as it works? No! It only usually matters when it's broken. We are going to explore such theories on life in the following pages and analyze what benefits they could yield if properly applied.

If you are already familiar with concepts like 'vibration' and 'sub-atomic-reality attraction', then please do read on because I will attempt to give some of my own insights into this area, and maybe some different theories to ones you may already know of. If you are completely new to all this new-age stuff, then also read on because I attempt to break my opinions and theories into very easily digestible pieces so you can be brought up to speed quickly.

I will get into the details of these things later on, for now just try to open your mind to the possibility that you possess an awesome power within you that you're going to harness (and maybe even master) with time and practice.

One doesn't have to understand exactly which thoughts/emotions/beliefs/circumstances have to be present to achieve some desired result in order to obtain it. The focused *intention* of producing the result is *always* what mostly *causes it to happen*.

I only know the basics about how a car works (pistons compress gasoline and air, then a sparkplug ignites the mixture and the piston fires, that then moves some gears which turn and eventually transfer the force into your wheels) but I wouldn't be able to tell you what any other part does if pointed out to me under a car hood. However I can still drive (only an automatic and on the right side of the road; yes, slightly embarrassing!) and enjoy the benefits of the car. I also realize that I don't actually need any knowledge of the operation of a car in order to obtain its benefits. All I need to know operationally is how to convince my Loving Partner to chauffer me to a particular location.

The same logic goes for my suggested methods, philosophies, life-enhancing technologies and different potential points of view.

While reading this book, even if you don't understand a particular concept completely, try to approach everything with an 'I don't get it, but I'll try it anyway' attitude. It is the attitude that I've always tried to have. Whenever I approach any problem or issue, I make the initial assumption that I CAN overcome it, and then I simply start trying. The specific way in which I am to do it is then revealed to me as I start trying. Remember, *attitude* is everything.

So, now you know how to get the best results from the suggestions/strategies/methods in this book: Try them! Unless you're really keen and curious and simply must know the scientific basis and case studies to verify the efficacy of anything BEFORE you try it, otherwise, just dive right in and try some of the things I mention in the proceeding pages that make sense to you. And if you must, go and research the area in which you feel you need the most help. Then, try out some of the tips and hints you've learned yourself.

Remember, not everything is for everyone, only go with the hints and tips that feel *right for you*. I'm just trying to give you options and open you to new ideas; feel free to research anything I mention to your heart's content. In fact, this book encourages you to go out and do your own research on the discussed topics. This book is not intended as a Gospel, it is intended as a facilitator for the expansion of wisdom and consciousness.

Let me now give you some chapter primers, so you can jump straight to the Life Front that interests you most (or you feel you need most improvement in) if you wish to do so. This book is intended to have all the chapters act as self-contained units and don't necessarily 'flow' into each other. You can read everything I have to say about one area of life and skip another (possibly one which you think you're particularly Awesome at already) so you can target your progression in your areas of current (temporary) weakness; if you choose to.

Chapter Primers (like trailers for a movie...)

Chapter 1 - The nature of things...

In this chapter, I ramble on about what I think this reality we all share actually is. What is this all actually made of? Who/What is God? That's the kind of deep, philosophical stuff explored in this chapter.

Chapter 2 - Dwelling on what we don't want

The infinite consciousness does not see negation. Putting out a constant thought into the ether of something you definitely DO NOT want, actually causes it to happen. You've probably heard it before, but in this chapter I explore the specific reasons why it all makes sense to ME. It may give you another angle of looking at the whole matter and possibly even give you some new ideas to explore.

Chapter 3 - Upgrading and Maintaining your Temple

This one's about your physical and mental health. Dispelling some of the myths that fly around to line the pockets of fat cats is on the agenda. So is the concept of 'living healthy in spite of the world's negative programming and counter-intuitive systems'. Also explored will be: alkalinity, breathing, exercise and, of course, the Mind's effect on physical health.

Chapter 4 - Emotions

Why do we feel the things we feel? Is a feeling only a reaction to an event or circumstance, or are the events and circumstances a reaction to our feelings? Are we able to effectively filter and control the emotions we feel on a consistent basis? What are the emotions that debilitate us and what can we do about them? This chapter is about what we feel and how we can use what we feel to our advantage.

Chapter 5 - On Relationships

How you get on with the people in your life and the quality of those people is largely influenced by your mindset towards relationships. How do you relate to these people? How would they describe you in terms of how good of a friend/daughter/

father/aunt/employee/lover/husband/wife/etc you are? Life is too short and precious not to live it amazingly surrounded by your loved ones.

Chapter 6 - Money

Is money your main priority or your main worry? The answer to that question is directly correlated to the amount of money you currently have. Where do you physically keep your money? This chapter will explore how to set yourself up to constantly have an abundance of this stuff.

Chapter 7 - Faith, Destiny, and the Freedom of Choice

Are you actually choosing to do what you're doing? And even if you actually are, does it have any effect on the future which may, or may not, be predetermined? How are you supposed to know what your destiny (or purpose) in this life is?

Chapter 8 - My Revelations

This chapter is about some of my views on the world and personal revelations I have had over the years. There will be the odd cliché, and I will probably be promoted to 'Captain Obvious' for some of my views. Can the world be saved? If so, what must we do to save it?

Sometimes all it takes is to be reminded of a great truth we already knew in order to develop and grow. Hey is that another revelation? Does that count?

How much can I expect to improve in each area?

I can't give you a specific answer. Every person is different, as is their own respective need (want) for change in their life. What I CAN tell you, is the minimum and maximum the average person *should* improve in each area after reading this book.

Let's assume that the average person is using exactly half of their potential in the main areas in life.

I foresee that the absolute *minimum improvement* in *each* area for the average person would be 10%; and this would only happen if you approach this book completely pessimistically and sceptically. This improvement will happen even if you don't use any of my suggestions at all.

So where would this improvement come from, you ask? Simply because some of my ideas, distinctions and ramblings will naturally permeate your subconscious and the slight changes will manifest in a gradual and subtle way.

This alone, translates into a significant *overall* improvement in your life. And keep in mind that this is my estimated minimum. There is no real maximum, the maximum improvement, is that you will approach 100% human potential. I only say *approach* because I believe that 100% human potential is no longer actually human; but instead, some sort of ethereal and God-like creature. And if you eventually become such a creature, then all the power to you!

What I hope for you, kind reader, is that my words will at least start you on the path towards achieving your own optimum trajectory of potential.

Remember, that this book simply tries to convey some concepts and ideas that will hopefully trigger you to go on your own journey of discovery; whether in an overall life improving way, or in a specific area that you want most to improve or that ignites your interest.

Be your own mad scientist experiment! (...about the format of this book)

Not in a weird, late night movie kind of way; in the life-improving way.

Every chapter will have one or more 'experiments' that you can actually try out for yourself. Approach all of these with an open mind and a can-do attitude. They are designed to be easily performable. They usually indicate an experiment length (usually 14 days), but feel free to try them for longer if desired.

You don't have to do the experiments in the order provided, or do all of them if you're already a mind guru. Also, don't limit yourself to the list, make your own experiments to hone your mental and physical skills; these are just a few suggestions you may not have considered.

If this book only makes you think about looking at your life (or a particular area) in a different way, then at least you've grown and developed. However, most of the 'theory' in this book is most effective when it's actually put into 'practice'.

Whenever I read a self-help book when I was younger, I would never actually use the tools that were suggested; I simply imagined doing it and assumed that I got the same benefit. Trust me when I say that there is no substitute to actually 'doing' what you 'think' you can/should be doing.

Feel free to combine any of the experiments and make your own unique 'life-improving-synergistic-experiment-combo'!

So open your mind and try some of my self-improvement experiments today!

A.L.O.A.F

This book is written with the following theory in mind; if one makes slight improvements in all the major areas of life, and in each area uses both practical (logical, scientific) and metaphysical (hippie-ish, unexplainable) approaches, then the overall life improvement would be far greater than the sum of their parts.

Try not to *just* focus on the practical or new-age stuff, try a bit of both. The point after all, is to not neglect any part of life, while striving to improve ALL of them at once. Obviously you may want to primarily focus on one, which is fine, but at least try *everything* from all angles on that one area. Try attacking it every way you can, and use everything that works for you in conjunction with everything else that works.

I personally try to 'maintain' everything at once (make sure it's all at a standard that I am 'happy' with) and put in all the 'progress and development' into an area that's either lacking, or an area that currently motivates or inspires me. At the moment, if you must know, I am currently mostly focused on getting a six-pack.

Which, notice, is a lot different than focusing on 'losing my gut'; as it is goal-oriented and positive, and doesn't give attention to the fact that I may have too much stored fat around my midsection. A very important distinction to make as you will see later on in the book. I am working on this goal from every angle I can think of.

I am blasting my brain with positive beliefs about my chiselled stomach. I'm doing crunches to strengthen and tighten the underlying muscles. My diet is also getting tweaked to include even more deep greens than usual. Also, I'm increasing my cardio gradually to decrease my overall body fat. Finally, I do static abdomen flexes whenever I get a chance throughout the day.

From this, you can see how I'm attacking just one goal from many different angles to drastically increase chances of success. I expect to have this 'six pack' in the next couple of months. Any goal in any area of life becomes a piece of cake if you attack it from all angles.

So without further adieu, prepare to *Attack Life On All Fronts!*

(I'm assuming you're getting that warm feeling you get the first time someone says the title of the movie in that movie.)

Banquet of Thought and Feeling

I welcome you now, to feast mentally with me.

On the menu, we have a main course of (hopefully) useful hints, side order of life-improving strategies, lightly seasoned with mostly useless, yet thought-provoking ramblings.

To wash all that down, we have some (hopefully) amusing anecdotes and observations.

Finally, for dessert we have a delicious selection of inspiration, motivation and hope.

Generous servings of Love will ensue throughout the meal.

This meal is not for the feint-minded or feint-hearted; I invite you to come mentally and emotionally starved.

Bon Appétit!

Section 1 – The Nature of Things

How it all began...

Firstly, there was a Big Bang. Believers: pay attention, because this is the part that 'God created the Heavens and the Earth'. Just for clarification I will be using mostly scientific terms to describe the dynamics of reality, but only for simplicity's sake; feel free to establish parallels to any piece of scripture that you happen to believe in. You can put whatever label on it, suffice it to say that at some point long ago, this particular universe started to exist. Whether through the Will of a divine entity or through a sequence of random cosmic events, ethereal 'mind stuff' started to organize into what we perceive as 'matter'. However you personally choose to interpret 'what' happened is correct, for you.

It is not my mission to debunk any religious beliefs or to shit on Faith in general, as Faith is an integral part of getting what you want from this universe. I am simply trying to spread enlightenment across the cosmos. Please note that enlightenment has different degrees, so there is no need to strive for a state of 'complete' enlightenment, as it is more of a journey than a destination. Unless, of course, you think you may be the next incarnation of The Buddha. I cannot tell you what road you should travel to reach spiritual, mental, and emotional fulfilment, as each road is individual to the individual soul. All I'm trying to do is show that there are countless ways of being and thinking, and that a person should try as many of these as possible until they find their own unique way which suits them specifically.

"Do not go where the path may lead, go instead where there is no path and leave a trail."

- Ralph Waldo Emerson

The point is that everyone could be right about the 'what' that happened, and that the 'how' and 'why' are subject to personal point of view and interpretation. So we can all use different words and pictures to *represent* the same phenomenon.

The most important thing to note is that we <u>are</u> here. Whether life on this planet started as a result of chaos or orchestrated intention is irrelevant.

The first way of looking at it states that this planet is simply a statistical anomaly; like if the truth was that one in every several million planets has the atmospheric/surface elements necessary to create life (and eventually intelligent life) and all you need is a catalyst (e.g. an asteroid impact, electrical storms, solar flares, etc.) to kick off the first living cells. That we are simply an accident (as if the universe forgot its pill or its condom broke).. I don't know about you, but even if this is the case, it doesn't make me feel like any less of a miracle.

The second option we could explore is that some external force seeded our planet with life. Whether that is an ethereal being which bestowed part of its consciousness into the first living cells, or a physical alien race genetically implanted life here is another tangent of debate. In any case, it would imply that there was an outside intelligence which *intended* for us to live. And also in this case, I feel equally as special and blessed that I have been allowed to have the *experience of life*. There are nearly endless permutations of circumstances around our creation, and not enough time to explore them all. You can debate which one of these scenarios gave rise to our existence until you're blue in the face.

However, unless you're high and/or enjoy this sort of philosophical deliberation, it will just probably drive you insane. It did me for a while several years back. In my belief, which one of these events happened isn't really important. Whichever way; we are a unique species, and even by our current 'logic' our very existence is a 'miracle'. Whether it's a statistical or divine one, is up to your own interpretation. And what if they're both actually the same thing?

The important thing is that we are here now and must make the most of it. We are equally blessed if we are just a statistical improbability or purely the will of God. Each one should give us reason to rejoice.

What our world is made of...

When we look around us, all we see with our eyes is matter. We see the ground, buildings, trees, cars, people, TV's, Mp3 players, beer bottles, drugs, computers, etc. All of these are made of matter which we can usually smash into tiny little bits if we wanted to. That is as far as our eyes go. We are only able to see particles as small as a grain of flour with the naked eye. This is where technology comes in.

We then need a normal microscope to be able to see smaller particles and molecules. We then get another kind of microscope which uses some cool technology to see further and see atoms and parts of atoms. Then we have to visit a high-tech research facility which has an even better microscope, and we see the bits of the atom are actually a localized field of energy vibrating. I know it's sometimes hard to accept and believe, and yes, getting a bit high before trying to grasp it helps.

"You don't have a soul. You are a Soul. You have a body."

- C S Lewis

Simply put, we are a localized field of consciousness (information), then a field of vibrating energy, then an atom, then a molecule, then a cell, then a physical organism. "So what?" you may be asking at this point. Well simply accepting the fact that there is no 'matter' as such, and that we are all simply experiencing the ever-changing dynamic 'mind stuff' according to our subjective awareness could have great ramifications in our lives. It would at least shift our perception.

If we could at least utilize a small portion of the understanding about life on all these levels, we would be able to tap into an unlimited power.

Over the years, humanity has researched the link between our physical existence and our conscious (and subconscious) thoughts. Despite what the 'logical' sceptics say, for me, this link is undeniable. It is a lot easier to live in ignorance of such high-level concepts, but for me, it is also a lot more boring.

Perception is everything

There are many ways this existence can be perceived. In fact, there are as many unique ways as there are minds walking the earth. Well, technically, everything has 'awareness' at some level, whether it is 'conscious' in the conventional sense or not. Let's not forget that most sentient beings also change their perception of their own existence throughout that existence. It is a necessary part of survival and evolution.

Since one can only truly know one's own perceptions, I have categorized some of mine I've had over the years.

Womb Perception: It's warm and I'm just floating around here. What am I? Who cares, I'm comfy.

Infant Perception: Everything's fun and new. I want to learn things. Why is everybody smiling at me? I don't really care 'what' I am. Everybody is minding me... I must be amazing to them.

Naive Child: Everybody else must feel like I do. Why are people hurting other people? Everybody loves me. Nothing can go wrong.

Disappointed Child: The world is a contraption built to spite me. Why can't I have everything that I want? Why am I being told that life is tough? Why was I made if all I do is what I'm told?

Evil Egoist: I am smarter than them. The world was made only for me, only to serve MY whims. I will manipulate this reality, to suit my needs. Since these selfish urges exist, it's God's fault for giving me them. If he wanted me differently he would've made me differently. I blame everyone but myself for all my problems, for some reason the problems don't seem to be going away. It's a cruel world, so I must be even crueller to be happy.

Paragon Wannabee: My mind is a gift from a creator. It is to be used to help others. Still a part of me wants to be well-off as well. Helping others feels good, so therefore isn't selfless. Is it possible to be addicted to generosity?

Objective'ish: We are a bunch of scalar, standing waves of information taking shape through energy vibrations. We are all consciousness, therefore we can (and should) experience anything and everything we want. The only fundamental choice to make is between Love and Fear; and my subjective view is that when you consider the logical outcomes, Love is the obvious one to choose.

The last category is where I've been for about seven years now, and going strong. There are an infinite amount of ways to perceive our reality, so feel free to change yours as often as you require. Every change in your life will result in firstly changing a perception (interpretation/belief). Try as many different points of view as you want, and use the ones that work for you.

"What is mind? No matter. What is matter?
Never mind. Hahaha"
-Homer Simpson quoting George Berkeley

Consciousness exists on all levels. You wouldn't usually think about all your body's cells as being 'conscious', but they are. Through scientific analysis, we can now see that individual cells actually communicate with each other, interact, and have the ability to organize and strategize.

There is a part of **your** consciousness that exists in each and every one of your cells, and another part of your consciousness that exists as part of the global collective consciousness. Most of us are only aware of 'I the human' awareness, without taking into consideration the 'I the billions of living cells' or 'I the part of all terrestrial consciousness'. All these scalar levels of consciousness are what keep all 'matter' in the universe together.

Animals seem to have this gift, they are aware of themselves as the animal, the billions of cells, and the part of all life. This is what gives rise to the phenomenon we call 'instinct'. If we, as humans, were able to experience the total awareness of all the levels of consciousness, I believe we would reach the pinnacle of our evolution (or at least the next big step). The actual methods and procedures to reach such awareness are unique to the person.

The way I see it, if your physical reality was a ship on the ocean; your conscious thoughts are your captain (decides where you want to go), your subconscious is your navigator (knows the way to your dreams), the infinite consciousness is your engineer (empowers you to get there, and does what it's told), your experiences in your life are the crew (all do their part to empower you to learn and grow), and your desired dream or goal is your 'Land ho!' You only get there when everyone on the ship does their job.

My take on Parallel Universe Theorem...

Imagine time flowing down like a river heading towards the future. Every decision anyone makes or any result that could have multiple outcomes makes different branches off that river, all flowing towards the future but along slightly (or dramatically) different paths. So whenever you said, 'I wonder what would've happened if I did THAT instead of the other', it DID happen, but in another reality (parallel world). There is another version of you in existence somewhere who made completely different choices than the ones you have made up till now. I still don't know whether these parallel worlds actually occupy the same space that we do, but are somehow just 'out of phase' with our current reality (the world behind the world), or are they all within our ONE universe but millions of millions of light-years away. I guess it doesn't really matter, all that matters is that they do exist somewhere, I don't have to know exactly where.

What I do know, is that there is a 'you' out there who ended up becoming a crack-head, smackhead, alcoholic, criminal or even God-forbid: a politician. The obvious reverse to that is that there is a 'you' out there who cured cancer in another world, or became a wealthy businessman, or a gold-medal athlete, or is whatever you currently want to be. The trick here is to remember that there are INFINITE combinations and permutations of the person that *you can be* just as there are INFINITE parallel worlds. For example, there is a parallel you out there who is a loving philanthropist, but is fat and unhealthy. There is another who is the reverse, and another who is slightly fitter, and another who lives two streets (cities/countries) down from you, and another......etc.

The point is, depending on where YOU CHOOSE to have your habitual conscious and subconscious thoughts, is where your mind will 'teleport' you. If you believe that you should be living a certain life, then believe it enough and you will harmoniously synchronize yourself with that particular reality (or parallel world). There is constantly going to be a 'better' version of you who you want to aspire to be, this is called progress and is as vital as breath. If you're not progressing, you are actually degenerating; stagnation is an illusion: Nothing actually ever stays the same for long, and we sometimes only see the progressive damage much later.

Sorry, if this is all a bit down-to-earth for you. Please allow me to abstract the entire matter out a bit.

Influence Space and Time

Yes, it's that 'vibration', 'quantum physics', 'thought manifestation' stuff again. Everyone has an event, or many, that has occurred in their past that started as a clear conscious thought some time before it occurred. It's time to face our quasi-reality! I'm not saying that you **must** believe this in order to be happy, it is simply offered as an alternative in case your current way of thinking isn't making you happy currently.

If nothing else, you should at least consider the option that *how you think affects how you live.*

You may not be new to the concept of thoughts altering physical reality; however I believe they can alter time as well. I believe that the Infinite Consciousness doesn't care about time and can even alter our past to manifest future results without our conscious awareness. *The mind-stuff that our physical reality is made of rearranges itself optimally to reflect your beliefs.*

If we were to at least understand and know how to implement a fraction of a percent of this power, we would indeed realize that we are all, in fact, God-like creatures. Feel my wrath puny mortals! I am in tune with the universe, I will influence my own and all your physical realities! MuahahahA!

cough Sorry... about that, I guess I went a bit power-mad for a second.

Make sure that doesn't happen to you. You may alienate yourself from others if you're constantly talking about 'spacey' things. It is really good from time to time to delve deep into such things; but remember that some people aren't even ready to hear these truths. Also do not forget that the point of the life experience is to enjoy and expand it. So do not cut off contact from those in your life who you Love just because they're not intellectually ready to hear these things or they're simply uninterested. I guarantee you will always find at least a couple of people with whom you can have the deepest and most profound conversations about altered realities and the like. You need the other 'grounded' ones to make sure YOU don't float off into space and neglect your physical experience.

Make sure you immerse yourself in the physical enjoyment from time to time. Seize every sensation of the physical moment. What proportion of time you allocate to living the physical and what proportion to floating around the Astral Planes is up to you. Tinker with it, and fluctuate that proportion according to what feels right to you.

Attack any of your limiting perceptions on all Fronts!

What is God?

Let me first begin by saying it is not my intention to offend or ridicule anyone of any faith. If you have strong (or fundamentalist) religious views, you may want to skip this entire section. I don't want to be branded a heretic and set atop a bonfire in the name of your God.

With that little disclaimer out the way, let us examine my take on this elusive character. Note that I will be referring to things as they **are** according to me, and in your reality they may **not be**; so remember that this is my opinion and my own interpretation.

Our God is the collective intelligence that surrounds and penetrates the earth, or indeed any planet with a species with conscious and subconscious thought. Our God is the ethereal internet that surrounds the planet, connects us all to each other, and knows everything that *was, is*, and *can possibly be*. This localized field of infinite intelligence is our Father, and the spirit within the centre of our planet is our Mother (Gaia).

The surrounding field of energy and the core energy are what are considered the 'Ying' and 'Yang'. They are both important, and one cannot exist without the other.

I believe that our localized field is also actually part of the infinitely large field (*The One God*) which takes up its own dimension: A dimension of pure Love and thought. This has been referred to as the 'super-conscious capability', 'universal mind', and 'infinite intelligence' to name a few. It is the single source of all creation and what we deem 'existence'.

The closest tangible thing we have on this physical Earth currently is Google. It is spread across the entire planet, it has a network that connects (on the level of communication) anyone to anyone else, and it has basically every fact, fiction, speculation, opinion, piece of useful information or nonsense and, of course, pornographic picture that has ever been produced.

God is a lot better though. There are still some God-forsaken lands where Google just doesn't reach. The connections of Google are limited by many man-made factors like: screen size (how many friends can you chat to at once?), bandwidth (internet speed), etc. Finally, God knows ALL, not just what has been produced, but EVERYTHING that has ever occurred, is occurring, and can occur. Only God knows the next hottest thing to be invented or to become popular. To top it all off, God is willing to share this information; we only need to know how to ask correctly.

God knew about the Internet when the world was all kings and peasants toiling in fields. Why did God not tell anyone? Simple, the world was not enlightened or intelligent enough to handle it. Natural progression of a civilized society had to be maintained. Think about it, if there suddenly was a jet engine in the Middle Ages, people at the time would be shocked and panicked. There would probably be a cult formed to worship this 'metal spinney spiral god'. If a major advancement in ploughing fields is made, however, people sit and marvel at the genius of the person who tied a piece of iron to the back of a horse. 'That person' tends to be the person that's most tapped into the infinite intelligence or God. That's not necessarily the person who is most 'morally good' or 'meek' or 'Godly' in the normally accepted meaning of the word. It is simply the person who is mostly attuned to picking up the right 'frequency' from the God Network and asking it the right question.

The reason that religious 'prayer' works (if the person has sufficiently strong conscious and subconscious belief in their respective 'God') is the same reason that secular (or atheist) visualisations/ hypnosis/subliminals work. The reason is your mind sending the same kind waves of vibrations and feelings of certainty. The difference is quite trivial, atheists believe that they are responsible for everything that happens around them and that their mind will help them to find resources or circumstances to achieve their goals; Believers believe that God will show them the way. Strong enough practice with either will get you the results you want, however the atheist will have a much harder time doing it. This is simply because intellectual analysis and logical deduction require much more mental energy to be expended than blind faith. If it gets you the desired results, stick with it and don't question 'why' all the time. Choose an angle (or angel) from which to look at life, and then *believe* in it!

"Being on the fence your whole life will just leave you with a sore bum"

-Me

I'm arguing a side which I think is currently quite rare. I'm daring to say that EVERYONE IS RIGHT! We all believe in the same thing, we just use different words to describe it.

Now can we please just learn to get along and chill the f*&k out?!

The world's major religions are all right: There is a God who watches over us and is omnipotent and knows all. He is the source of all intelligence and relatively primitive humans like us would not be able to fully comprehend his true nature. Unless you're killing in his name, what could be the harm in believing in a great wisdom source (ethereal father figure) that watches over us and is the source of all that is good?

Pagans/Hippies are right: At the core of the Earth exists Gaia, the spirit of our planet which manifests on the surface as Nature. Our Mother nurtures us and helps us grow. Sure, there might have been some blood sacrifices to nature Gods long ago; but nobody recently has died from groups dancing around naked in a grove. Again, if it compels you to Love all creatures of the planet and have a deeper understanding of existence, then what could be the harm?

Atheists (the smart ones) are right: We are just people who live and breathe, but have a part of our brain which is unique in its ability to (somehow) link us on a subconscious level to a source of infinite intelligence/universal mind/(fill in your own scientific term) which modern science is not yet able to fully explain or comprehend.

So you see, there is no such thing as a true atheist, because even science admits it doesn't yet know everything. Therefore would it not be logical to call every current scientific mystery 'God's domain'? I think so. Some people that are 'strong atheists' profess to 'knowing' that there is no God. But to make such an assumption, one would have to 'know' *everything* that there ever is, was or ever will be known. A rather arrogant assumption to make; not even I would make such a boast. There is an undeniable amount of 'reasonable doubt'; therefore, logically, the unknown cannot be discounted as a factor.

Now that I think about it, I think people who consider themselves strong atheists have a sadder existence. They don't think anybody is watching over them, which to me, seems like a rather depressing outlook on life. But hey, to each their own, some people simply like to believe that their conscious mind is the only thing that affects what they do in life. They obviously are able to find joy in different things than I. This is good, for if a couple of atheists take offence at me saying that they have a 'sadder existence', they won't assassinate me in the name of their God. ☺

You may be thinking that I'm being a hypocrite in arguing both sides of the coin. But I have decided; I have decided that both versions are in fact of the same phenomenon. My decision is that *it doesn't actually matter;* as long as your interpretation of God doesn't lead you to do 'evil' in its name, then it is right.

Therefore it is needless for me to bet for either Science or Religion. I believe that one should A.L.O.A.F. and take the bits that feel the best from every angle. There will be times and situations, I believe, that would benefit from a purely logical (atheistic) view point; while there will be others that will have the most beneficial outcome if looked at from a more 'divine' point of view.

Good and/or Evil?

Do these things truly exist? I believe that the perception needs to exist for Good or Evil to exist. We need to realize that these are just concepts that we use to represent the ends of the 'vibration scale'. The concepts are then twisted and perverted until they simply serve the goal of the accuser.

Let's take a very simple example. A poor and starving father breaks into a house to steal some food for his starving family. (Good, from his family's point of view) He is heard breaking in the back door in the night by the man of the house. (He is perceived as an Evil burglar) The starving father is shot to death by the frightened man of the house. (Split public opinion on who was Good and who was Evil) So you see; these are dynamic labels which change depending on the view of the observer.

Think about it; who we *should* perceive as 'evil' people are just ones who spend most of their time being in a 'low vibration'. Are those 'evil' dictators far away actually happy? No! They spend all their time and energy on war, greed, power, money, and fear of losing it all. The only thing that gives them temporary release from their misery is quelling a revolution, getting arms shipments, or expanding their territory. It's absolutely pointless. It is living with a constant and ever-growing hunger. To dwell in hatred and fear is the true evil as I understand it.

The most these people deserve is our pity. They do not deserve our fear, our loyalty or even our attention. Even if they had all the power/money/land in the world, they would not be satisfied. Even the Emperor in Star Wars would have nothing to do if he managed to quell the rebels. He would be left with a distinct feeling of 'is this all there is?' I bet even total galactic domination would not actually make him happy and fulfilled; he would keep wanting more and fearing more until the day he died. Luckily, Anakin finally realized the folly of following the 'Dark Side' and took the Emperor out of his misery.

How about 'evil' actions? Remember that these labels require perception. One person may see the same thing as 'good' as many others will deem 'evil'. Remember also, that not too long ago, in certain places, a woman could be deemed 'an evil witch' and burned at the stake completely arbitrarily.

There isn't really any *true* evil; there is only 'generally-accepted' evil.

I believe that truly **evil** action is one that either lowers your own vibration or contributes to the overall lowering of the Earth's (or Universe's) vibration. You heard what these things are all your life. Whatever your faith, you must've got some guidance on what actions to avoid in your life: Don't kill, don't steal, don't lie, don't be greedy, etc. These are the obvious basics, but they should not be taken as gospel.

The good news is you don't really have to learn anything new to avoid low-vibration actions. Just acknowledge that you have been avoiding low vibration actions without needing to know they would 'lower' your or the Earth's vibration. The general rule one could follow to determine the 'goodness' of any action is:

In the deepest part of my being (soul, core), do I truly believe this action will enhance my (or everyone's) vibration level?

Remember, however, that we both need 'light' and 'dark' energies to be in balance. You're not going to get anywhere in life if you're overly kind and nice to everyone all the time. People will start taking advantage of you and you will be considered a push-over. There may be times when it's actually 'right' to lie/cheat/steal/kill. Don't ask me to list any examples, because these are going to be individual for YOU. If you truly believe in your core that a 'dark energy' action is required to elevate the vibration level of all concerned, then your integrity will guide you to the best course of action.

We were all blessed with one amazing thing: Free Will. You can choose to let low or high vibrations dominate your life. However, also acknowledge that trying to completely eliminate low vibrations is self-defeating. Simply focus on living in the peak/high-energy/high-vibration/loving/grateful/wise part of life, and the low will naturally be kept at bay. Let us never deny our dark side's existence in all of us, lest it take us unaware. Complete dominance of either side is not beneficial, for both are needed to grow and survive in this physical reality.

Now that we have a grasp of some basic concepts, let's dive right into how to shift your thinking to improve and expand your life experience.

Section 2 – Using Universal Truths to get what you want in your current manifestation of consciousness (Life)

The Evidence

If you're anything like me, you need to at least see some proof of something before you go and start believing it or considering it as a possibility. Since all these theories of quantum physics are yet to be precisely and fully defined, we must take some little leaps of faith. However, if you look at the anecdotal and 'derived' evidence you'll see that it just makes sense and you don't actually have to put that much blind faith into it. If you look at the following points, you will quickly realize that there is a pattern emerging and there is 'something to all this new-age stuff' after all. At the very least, consider the following scientifically-documented anomalies:

- **Random number generators influenced by thoughts**
  Feel free to Google this one. There are studies which prove that, at least to some degree, our thoughts can physically alter something as sophisticated as computer circuitry to give us a desired result. If something that intricate can be so precisely manipulated at a sub-atomic level, imagine how easy it would be for the Universe to give you something as crude as a house or some money.

- **Nerve cells connected across distance by unknown force**
  Research this one as well. It seems a study has been done where a subject's live nerve cells (out of his mouth, I think) where exposed to electric shocks while being hundreds of miles away from the subject. The subject's attached nerve cells reacted in a way as if they, themselves, were shocked. This proves to me that there must be a field of consciousness (or information) that lies beyond our atoms. To me, this means that all of our cells have consciousness at some level. This leads me to the conclusion that since all matter is conscious at some level, it must be vulnerable to influence by consciousness itself.

- **Goggles that turn your world upside down**
  This is a study where a group of people were given goggles which inverted their world. After about 28 days, the first of the group experienced a phenomenon, after 35 days, the entire group did. All their brains, rewired themselves to compensate for the inverted image and they started seeing normally through the goggles. This just further proves to me the immense power of our brains.

- **My Super Computer Powers**
  I have always been interested in computers, but when I was around twelve I think I developed some sort of ethereal bond with them at a subconscious level. Since that time, I've always fixed computers effortlessly. Often people will ask me how to solve an error message, and when I get to the computer everything works fine and the person cannot get the error while I'm there. Yes, I realize I may be having delusions of grandeur. However **this** is exactly how I believe people develop every lasting belief: They have one (often several) experience (positive or negative) which they choose to interpret as representing some pattern of outcome/behaviour and start saying things

like "I'm always good at [that]" or "[this] always happens to me". That phrase then gets repeated consciously and subconsciously. Before you know it you start believing you have unearthly luck, mental powers, a 'knack' for always doing getting x, etc. It is then perpetuated as your thoughts attract more that is in line with this belief.

- **The Placebo Effect**
  Why does this happen? This is undeniable evidence of the whole mind-matter connection, yet it seems largely overlooked by 'realists'. I'm not suggesting we try it, but I reckon that a widely-publicised (fake) magic disease-curing pill would actually cure all the patients that were particularly susceptible to this effect. I have a strong belief that any 'conventional' medicine also only works if we have a mind set on convalescence.

- **Thank you/Idiot Rice Jar**
  Do this experiment yourself. Take two identical jars of cooked rice, label one 'Thank You' and one 'Idiot' or 'Asshole' or some other negative word that you hold in low esteem. Every day say *Thank You* to the Thank You jar and say a couple of obscenities to the Idiot jar. See what happens after several days.

- **Vegetarians as cruel as carnivores?** This was an experiment done by some scientist a little while back. If I had any doubt about the consciousness of everything, I would try to re-create this experiment for myself. Maybe you can give it a try yourself too.

  Basically, two house plants, several feet away from each other were hooked up to stress sensors (polygraphs). The scientist then comes into the room and rips one plant into bits. Swearing, cutting and tearing at its green flesh. After some time, the scientist returns to the room... yup, you guessed it; the remaining plant's polygraph is going off the chart. It was obviously scared (or at least conscious of danger) and stressed at some level by the scientist's presence.

There are many more pieces of 'evidence' to the whole mind-matter connection thing, so go and research them if you're still not convinced. This list is by no means exhaustive to the amount of proof I have researched and witnessed in all my days. If you're still being all 'realistic' (sceptical, logical, intellectual) about it, ask yourself one question: *Would it really hurt to try thinking from a different perspective to see if it will improve my life experience?*

Before you start the war, you must plan out the objectives. Choose the ground you wish to win and attack it full force. Remember however, that our only enemy is our disbelief in our own potential.

What do you F@&ing want?*

You've heard it before and you'll hear it again: Do you know what you truly want? So many people (assuming they already truly know) will just brush over this quickly and then go into an entire essay about all the things wrong, all the obstacles in the way, and all the things they DON'T want but for 'some reason' they keep getting. I know they're all over and they're in your face, and they keep reminding you of what you don't want and what you should complain about. Listen, I understand, and I feel what you're thinking. Take it from someone that has been the MOST pessimistic, cynical and negative person imaginable that you CAN defeat it. This is the trick to the whole thing; shift your habitual energy from focusing on what you currently have (or do not have) to where you want to be and what you WANT TO have.

There are things you can do which will help you to achieve this. Consciously catching yourself when you're being negative when you can be choosing a more positive interpretation is definitely a start.

The aim is to get to a point, where, as soon you catch yourself dwelling on anything that may not be so perfect in your life; you interrupt your current pattern and consciously start focusing on all the awesome things that you have to be grateful for. I know, I know... it does seem hard at first. I do understand, this was tremendously difficult for me to achieve at first. I kept thinking that only 'doing' more and different things would produce different results. I completely failed to see that physical things and circumstances can (and do) change of their own accord, once the observer's focus (point of view, perception) changes.

So, once you master the art of constant conscious happiness, there is still that huge bit of the mountain to conquer which is your subconscious. Queue Mr. Reticular Activating System! This little guy is the physical part of your brain which will sit in the background and work diligently to seek out the circumstances and information that it has programmed into it. Are you ready to utilize this guy to his full potential? If so, try the following experiment.

The Subconscious Mind-hacking experiment

Commit to blasting your mind with positive ideas and attitude for the next two weeks. While you're consciously trying to sort out things in the physical realm, put your subconscious to work for you.

Step 1 – Get the kit

Firstly, you must have a way to access your subconscious mind to program your RAS. I think the best way to do this is to combine Audio and Visual Subliminals. Get yourself a cool little program (there are several out there) which flashes text messages taken from a list of affirmations (you can make your own list too!) for a fraction of a second on your computer monitor; thus enabling you to passively hack your brain as you're playing/working on your computer at home and work.

Next, get yourself some subliminal MP3s or download some software that allows you to record your own. A subliminal track is basically some cool music (that you hear) with spoken affirmations that you can't hear because they're recorded just outside of the range of conscious hearing. (i.e. your subconscious, and ONLY your subconscious can hear them [and maybe some dogs])

To saturate different parts of the mind further, I suggest surrounding yourself with imagery and symbols of your particular intention or goal.

I don't really advocate vision boards (ALL your goals as pictures on a board), although will agree with their efficacy. The problem is though; you won't know which goal your subconscious will work on attracting first. Chances are, you will eventually get everything on the board, but in how long and in what order may be 'random' in your eyes. If you focus on the ONE goal you currently want most, you will be sure of 'sniping' that particular goal and not 'AK47 – spraying and praying' your subconscious all over the place.

Step 2 – Program it

Now that you have the kit to open the backdoor into your operating system (mind), it's time to give it some commands. Make sure you have a good list of affirmations to program into your computer application and Mp3s. Also, make sure your pictures symbolize or actually depict the exact goal you have in mind.

Make sure your affirmations are in present tense, because that's the only way the subconscious mind thinks. Also make sure they are ONLY in the positive. And try to use words that have special meaning to you and evoke some emotional response if possible; this will further help to speed up absorption.

Some of my favourite affirmations:

I have the most amazing life partner in the world

I am an amazing specimen of human potential

I attack life on all fronts

I am wealthy financially, mentally and emotionally

I improve the world around me with my positive presence

I am extremely fit, healthy and energetic

I love everyone as part of me, and everyone loves me in turn

Step 3 – Cruise towards your dreams

Now, run your subliminal computer program to be always on for the next 14 days. If you can get away with it, put in on the computer at work as well. Make sure you don't have an overly-anal I.T. department if you want to do this.

Every day for the next 14 days dedicate to listening to the same one or two subliminal and/or hypnosis tapes at the same time of day. Putting it on 'repeat' mode before you go to sleep every night may be an option if you're feeling brave or silly. I found that a short tape (mp3 track actually) with upbeat music works well first thing in the morning, and a different type of tape with classical/nature sounds is amazing just before bed.

At every opportunity, look at the picture(s) or symbol(s) of your goal and take a few seconds to put yourself into that future state of feeling. Close your eyes and imagine what you will feel as a result of your goal coming to fruition.

Step 4 – Let it go

Don't dwell and deliberate on it after it's locked in. If you do, it may create doubt; what you want to do is proceed with life as usual with an attitude of positive expectation. After the two weeks are up, stop doing the process for this particular goal. Release your intention into the cosmos and trust that it's on its way. You should now take a couple of days break from the experiment and shift your focus onto something else. If you're feeling ambitious or antsy, you may restart the experiment for another goal.

If you still feel that you want to attack this from even more angles, then concurrently have a try with the following collection of little experiments - you can have fun with them during the course of your day.

On-the-go mind-hacking Experiments

Try out some of these experiments to hone your mental-to-physical manifestation powers. Do some of these trials yourself and become a believer in the infinite power of your own mind!

Experiment 1 – Get something small and tangible

This experiment involves focusing your conscious mind on some small token item that must appear to you in the near future. When you wake up in the morning, intend to acquire an item that seems insignificant and trivial to you but that you don't usually receive on a normal day. Make it something that you could go out and buy, so you know it's possible to have one, but would much rather it was just given to you out of the blue.

Make sure that it's an object that you don't have a phobia about, and would like to receive. However it's not something that you want to go out of your way to acquire, so it would be nice and convenient if one just magically appeared.

Keep it simple. Something like a particular chocolate bar, a flower, a cup of peppermint tea, a five pound (dollar) note, or a nice pen will do.

Now, first thing in the morning, and whenever you get a chance to throughout the day, picture receiving it out of the blue. Try to evoke and enhance the joyful feelings it creates when you receive it. Emphasize the gratitude towards the universe for giving you your desire. Obviously you may have to embellish how happy and grateful you will feel when you just get a simple cup of tea.

Do this for a couple days in a row. You may find you receive it during the course of the day in which you're trying to manifest it; however, you may get it a day or two later. If you do focus on it and believe it's possible, you will get it. Exactly *when* you'll get it is hard to tell. This isn't an exact science (yet).

Experiment 2 – Park despite all odds

The purpose of this experiment is to prove that we can influence 'circumstances' which are obviously dependent on countless physical factors with our minds.

Try to increase your 'hit rate' of getting a parking space to above 90% by simply visualizing the spot. Before you set out on your journey, keep the vision of the empty space in your mind. Visualize exactly where it's going to be, and that you will be there at the exact moment to pull into it. I personally have increased my success to about 92% in about one year.

Experiment 3 – Dream goal mission

This one is the longest term experiment, and will use all of your mind-hacking tools.

Program your subconscious kit (experiment before this one) to focus on only the object of your desire. Remember to program it all in the present (eg. I HAVE [that thing]).

Follow your subconscious-hacking routine religiously (or secularly) for the next two weeks. Also while doing this, put up pictures (I prefer copies of the exact same picture) of your object in various places around your house. One you can see just as you wake up is good. Another maybe by the bathroom mirror, as it's a place where most of us are semi-consciously brushing our teeth or shaving. Another still in the field of vision of your TV; because if you're a big TV watcher you're constantly being programmed by the damn box anyways, you might as well give your subconscious a chance to focus on your goal.

After the two weeks, release it all. Stop the subconscious routine and take down the pictures; pretty much forget about it and let the Universal Mind take care of it.

Of course, you can make your own experiments to see if your mind responds better to more/less saturation, shorter/longer experiment duration, more/less conscious affirmations, or perhaps a new object of desire that evokes more (or stronger) emotions.

Practice Gratitude

Now that you may have achieved something you 'wanted', it's important to see that it's not necessarily what you 'needed'. If you don't start to appreciate all the things you already have, you will spend your life in a constant state of hunger and/or overwhelming greed.

You've probably heard this a million times before, but I need re-emphasize the importance of it. The **simplest way** out of focusing on the negative is to consciously focus on all the things in that area for which we are grateful. This, if nothing else, will stop you from thinking about the particular negative in that moment. However it will not just do that, it will do a lot more. It will completely reverse your energy into a positive range, therefore creating a positive vibration out of something that originally took your attention as a 'negative'. This is one of the most powerful feelings to practice.

Have you ever noticed anybody that had much less than you physically, but seemed perfectly happy despite that? If you actually talk to them, you will notice that it is because they are grateful for the few things that they do have. They probably also define their happiness with more abstract things like peace, love and health, **not** how much money they have in their account or how much *bling* is swinging from their neck.

Here are some examples of negatives you could be dwelling on or worrying about, and their related things you should be grateful for instead:

Worrying Negative	Things you can focus on being grateful for instead
What if I lose my job?	• You are employed now • You have the opportunity to currently add value to the world in your working capacity • You've already accumulated experience to put on your CV (Resumé) • The job has already contributed to the development of your character
What if I get hit by a bus tomorrow?	• You are alive now • You have an amazing brain that will take care of you and could even relatively slow down time for you to respond in emergencies • Your knowledge and implementation of positive vibration makes your subconscious avoid such circumstances • You have the power within you right now to decide that only amiable and positive things happen to you

(Continued)

Worrying Negative	Things you can focus on being grateful for instead *(Continued)*
What if I stopped being loved by [insert loved one]?	• **They love you now** • **You are enjoying the love now** • **Your relationship is growing and expanding** • **You had a chance to experience this love in the first place (better to have loved and lost...)**
I don't have enough money	• **You have enough for food, clothing, and a roof over your head** • **Opportunities for making money are all around you** • **You probably have enough to buy a book that could change your life**
I think I'm too fat	• **You are still alive, so it's not too late to start living more healthily** • **You can still walk, thereby making it easier to burn it off** • **There are lots of people out there with a 'fat fetish', so you can still get some loving while you're getting fit**

Now that you've gotten the hang of finding things to be grateful for, let's look at replacing your negative internal monologue with new positive affirmations. Remember to always write and think about affirmations in the **present, and always in the positive.**

We'll use the same examples as before.

Worrying Negative	New Positive Affirmations to replace them with
What if I lose my job?	• I am secure in my employment • I am indispensable to the company • Everyone at work appreciates my contribution and positive attitude
What if I get hit by a bus tomorrow?	• I am always safe and secure • I have amazing longevity • My life will continue for many more decades (or centuries if you've just watched Highlander)
What I stopped being loved by [insert loved one]?	• This person loves me • I have an amazing, eternal relationship with this person • I love and appreciate this person
I don't have enough money	• I have money coming in from expected and unexpected sources • I have infinite abundance • I am a strong money magnet • I am immensely wealthy
I think I'm too fat	• I am chiselled and muscular (or toned and sexy) • I am in top shape • 1I am desired by all members of the opposite (or same) sex • I have *x*% body fat (where x is what you consider your ideal) • I'm able to lift *x* kilograms comfortably

Now start to habitually, consciously think about these (and your own) affirmations and incorporate them into your experiments.

The key to everything!

This is an all-encompassing philosophy. Accepting and believing these universal truths and distinctions will have a dramatic impact on *every* area of your life. Ever since I incorporated this way of thinking into my everyday life, I have seen all the pieces of my life puzzle almost fit in on their own. Once you decide which area of your life you wish to improve with a new positive outlook, you will immediately notice knock-on effects in other areas of your life.

Use this in any part of your life that you think is lacking. Simply appreciate all the things in that area that *are* going well and accentuate them. Then, practice 'pre-emptive' gratitude and start feeling the appreciation for the amazingly awesome things/circumstances/achievements that are already on their way to you.

Are you ready for a WAR?!!

I've devised a little model hierarchy of my 'war plan' to illustrate how I view personal development. Using the following figure, we see that we can achieve absolutely anything we want in our lives because we can break down any skill or mindset into easily-achievable chunks.

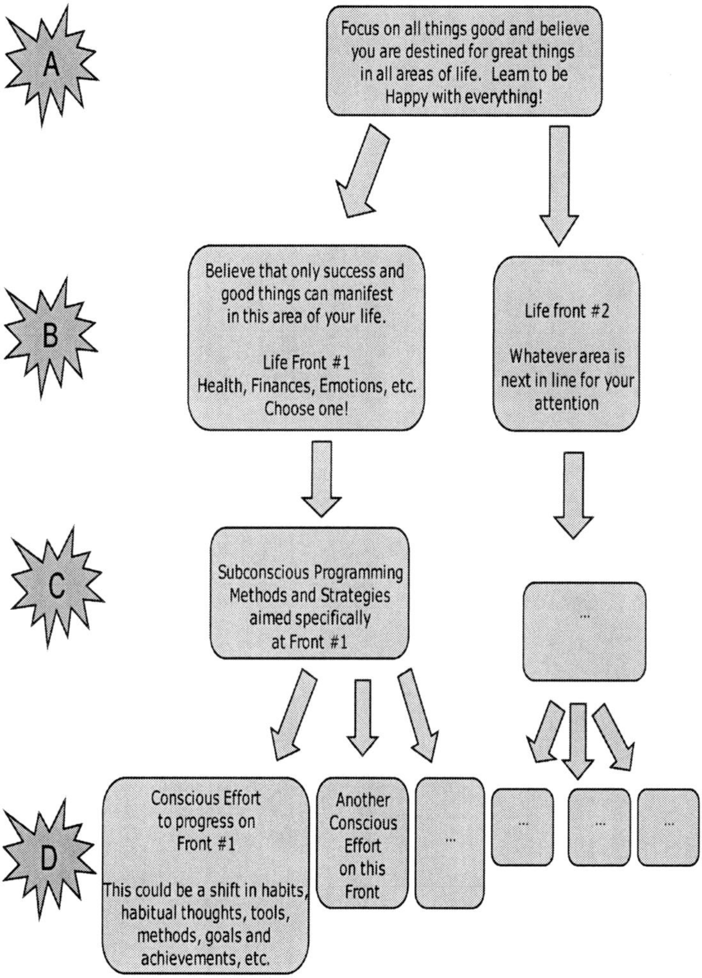

Looking at this model, we can see an 'attack' on a Life Front broken up into 4 levels (A, B, C and D).

You can look at it this way:

The 'D' level actions are your infantry; single-handedly they will not win you the war, but are crucial to your success and most effective in bigger numbers. You could say that the 'D' stands for 'Doing', as this is the level where you're actively taking conscious actions to improve your life.

The 'C' level is like your artillery; hugely effective, ranged, and mostly passive. They are closely linked with the 'D' level activities, as they are needed to make most of the headway on a Front, but still require the backup of 'D' level activities to put up the victory flag and hold the acquired ground.

The 'B' level is the Battle Level. Each Front is its own battle. However, by using your armies, the 'D' infantry and the 'C' artillery, you should be able to win any battle.

The 'A' level is the entire war. The prizes, of course being: true happiness, infinite love, enlightenment, etc. Basically, being more than content in every single aspect of your life.

Obviously, you cannot win the war unless you have won all the battles. So, depending on how you want to A.L.O.A.F., either focus all your attention on a single battle until you win and move on, or rally all your soldiers and cannons across all Fronts at once.

Too many people put up the white flag before the battle has finished. Believe me, if you can habitually change your ways of conscious and subconscious thinking, amazing things will manifest in your life effortlessly.

Now that we have some empowering beliefs as ammunition, let us mobilize towards attacking our first Front: Our physical and mental health.

Section 3 – Upgrading and Maintaining your Temple (... about health)

Legal Disclaimer: Statements and information regarding any products/diets/remedies mentioned within this chapter have not been evaluated by the Food and Drug Administration and are not intended to diagnose, treat, cure, or prevent any disease or health condition. By continuing to read, you are agreeing that you understand the contents of this disclaimer paragraph and release the author from any liability resulting from the application of the following content.

The main key to physical health is mental health

When your mind is at its peak, it's not being overworked, and it focuses on health; it's not possible to be physically unhealthy. If your mind is ill, then so will be your body. Let me clarify this, as you're probably saying 'Hey, I'm not a psychopath or schizophrenic, so why am I still sick with *x*?'

I'm not talking about just being in the range of socially accepted 'sane' people. I'm talking about being **free of all worry, stress, fear, negative thoughts and destructive emotions**. A little bit trickier, yes?

Other than maybe Buddha, I don't know of anyone that has ever achieved this perfect state. But don't despair, just try to be 'aiming for and approaching 100%' and I promise you that your physical body will thank you. If that seems daunting, just try to increase to the next 1%. After a while, the little bits of progress add up.

Life is often a trade-off; sometimes we must endure a little mental strain or stress in order to gain something that will hopefully make our lives less stressful in the future.

Definitely don't stress about not being able to eliminate all your stress. The following should be a question you should ask yourself when you're faced with a decision on whether or not you should do something that will potentially be stressful:

Is the stress (hassle, mental strain, effort) that this action/decision will cause me going to result in me having less stress in the future?

For example:

1. Going to work – Can be stressful (depending on your job and job satisfaction)

2. Not being able to pay rent – Very Stressful

Therefore it makes sense to endure the stress of #1 in order to avoid #2. Obviously the end result should be having a life in which there is always a stress-free or low-stress (everyone needs a little bit to keep life interesting) way out of any situation. Some stress is crucial, for it enables you to grow and develop; and you need to grow and develop to survive.

So free yourself from all negative thoughts and your body will definitely benefit. Stop worrying about things you cannot influence. ("When you worry you make it double") You may want to re-read the chapter on emotions (it's the next chapter actually) to further ingrain the concepts and notions that will help you to have a healthy mind. While you are minding your mind (I know) however, do not neglect your physical body:

It needs goods maintenance as well. Attack your health on all fronts!

Dare to go against your doctor's advice

First off, let me begin by saying that this is a very controversial topic and anything you try as a result of my 'alternative' opinions is AT YOUR OWN RISK. DO consult a physician if you are considering dramatically changing your diet or lifestyle. I am not claiming to diagnose or cure any disease. All I can do is share with you my own lifestyle choices and ways of thinking on this subject that personally work for me; what you do with them is completely up to you.

Now with that little disclaimer out of the way, let me be the first to tell you that conventional modern medicine is just flat out WRONG!

If you go to a doctor nowadays with any sort of ailment or discomfort, what would that doctor do? They would prescribe some sort of legal (or maybe sometimes illegal) drug that will apparently 'cure' you. In most cases these drugs will treat the symptoms but not the root CAUSE of the ailment. In the other cases they will actually make you worse.

Yay! You cured the inflamed knee joints, but now have a headache and diarrhoea! For which, you take some different antacids and painkillers, which have even more and elaborate side effects. Round and round the cycle of illness goes! Bottom line is that all of them contribute greatly to the overall toxicity of your blood and tissues.

The Alkaline/Acid school of thought says that the main factor that affects our health is the state of our Alkaline Buffering System. Simply put, it states that if you keep your blood and tissues at their optimal alkalinity (7.36 for blood), you will not be susceptible to **any disease.**

Since I started minding my alkalinity as my main health guide, I have not had so much as a cold for the last 4 years. Yeah, Really.

Proof of Alkalizing benefits

First off, go and find a video of Pleomorphism online, because this phenomenon which was previously deemed impossible was captured on film. Basically it shows a bacteria rod form transforming into a normal blood cell. Yeah, Really.

What does this mean? This means that the conventional paradigm about germs causing disease is seriously flawed. It shows that genes and life respond to the environment, not the other way around. We conventionally believe that because of the presence of certain organisms, we become sick. The sceptics will see the proof and still deny it. It is your choice, keep seeking more proof while dying of something preventable or open your eyes and use common sense.

Secondly, I've tried it and it works for me. That's the most convincing proof that I need to believe in this. It's not just me though; you'll see countless testimonies to back up the alkaline/acid approach to health. If anecdotal evidence is insufficient, then go find the raw data.

Research it yourself, the proof is out there. There are clinical trials with ionized water and cattle, which clearly show significant improvements in the milk quality and quantity. Animals are not subject to placebo effect, remember.

Eat or smoke the Greens?

The first (and probably biggest) step to becoming more Alkaline is adjusting your diet. I'm not saying go on a DIET, or completely flip your current one on its head. All I am saying is that you may need to adjust it slightly, bit by bit, until you have about an 80:20 (alkaline to acid, by volume) ratio in the foods you eat every day. It is *always* healthier to eat a green than to smoke one.

How do I achieve this in reality?

You don't have to be a green addict in order to drastically improve your health. Let's say that you eat on average 20 meals a week, and let's also say that they're all unhealthy (dead, acidic, processed or just plain junk). Now, imagine you were to replace 4 of these meals a week with healthy, alkaline meals. Firstly you would be taking away 4 acidic meals, which in itself would be beneficial; but also you would be adding 4 meals which would provide all the nutrients and alkalizing minerals that your body is probably lacking. The end result would be much more than a 20% increase in healthiness. (4/20 = 20%)

I know it may seem daunting, or even impossible, but believe me, if you start researching this particular topic you will soon realize how much crap you've put into your body over the years, and you will actually find it more difficult to stick to an unhealthy lifestyle. Because you will be in the know, and you will think twice about every piece of acidic food you ingest.

Acid Thoughts (No, not the LSD you did years ago)

Acid is also released as a result of negative thoughts and emotions. The more time you spend there moping, crying, being pissed-off, worrying, etc., the more acid you are releasing into your bloodstream. That may be hard to swallow at first, but rest assured this is the biggest factor contributing to your physical health.

A healthy mind will **always** have a healthier body than an unhealthy mind. The correlation can be seen in almost everyone you see. Now, is it the mind or body's turn first? The truth, as I understand it, is that the two are so deeply interconnected that affecting one will definitely affect the other. If you physically drink some booze, doesn't your mind wander off in directions it wouldn't normally? (Unless you're an alky of course) And don't you notice when your mind is focusing on stressful, negative things, it manifests in your physiology? You know: the slumped shoulders, shallow breathing, low-energy, and that unpleasant feeling in your stomach, tears?

The links are (to me) absolutely undeniable. So then, which do we focus on? The answer is *both!* We should simultaneously nourish and take care of both mind and body.

Attack acid toxicity on all fronts!

Breathe deeply now

This is probably the simplest and definitely the cheapest way to increase your overall health. Breathing correctly will ease your stress, lower your blood pressure, and stimulate your lymph. When we're babies, we know the proper way of breathing, but somewhere in growing up we lose the plot. We should breathe from the diaphragm, not the top of the lungs. Try it consciously, you'll notice a difference.

I guess the ideal would be to make it a habit again so that we use our oxygen intake most efficiently. Just one consciously-executed breathing exercise, however, will produce amazing instant results in that moment.

Breathing experiment

Try it yourself! Stick to the following routine for the next two weeks and see if you notice a difference.

One breath:

- Take about five to ten seconds to **fully** inhale; keep inhaling past the point where you'd normally stop

- Breathe from your diaphragm (abdomen)
- Hold the entire breath for between 15-20 seconds
- Exhale for a couple seconds longer than your inhale

One session:

Now, repeat that one breath 10 times (or 20 if you have the time and willpower, you can't over-breathe remember)

One day:

Aim for about 4-6 sessions a day.

One session in the morning, one before bed, and a couple during the course of the day.

Try it for the next two weeks, I guarantee you'll incorporate better breathing into your regular routine. Or if you don't, at least you'll know how good it can feel.

Also feel free to use it:

- Before an exercise session
- As you wake up
- Right before bed

- During that mid-afternoon energy slump
- Before or during a meditation session

You'll be amazed at what a difference a breath makes.

Wet Yourself... uhhhm, Hydrate Properly

Drink more water. You hear it all the time. What you should hear is: Drink more high quality alkalizing water. The quality and the amount are important. Personally, I don't believe there's anything better for you than structured, alkaline water. If you have lots of money, I recommend investing in an ionizer. If not, buy some lemons, and add the juice of one lemon to a bottle of Evian or Volvic. (Or preferred brand of bottled mineral water)

We need a lot more water than the typically recommended 8 glasses a day. I personally drink between 2.5 and 4 litres of water every day, and have felt amazingly better since I started this amount.

The self-hydrating experiment

If good water is good for us, then *awesome* water must be *awesome* for us. For the next 2 weeks, simply commit to drinking 5 alkalizing drinks every day, and taking away one daily acidic drink (You have to lose the can of cola or the morning coffee). What I mean by an *alkalizing drink* is 8 oz of:

- Purified water with some PH boosting minerals (in drops or powder)
- A Green Drink (freeze dried grasses and green juices, reconstituted with water)
- Ionized Alkaline Water: An ionizer will set you back between 1000-3000 dollars (600-1500 pounds), but if you can afford it, this is the most efficient way to get the healthiest water available to you
- Water with the juice of half a lemon in it (Yes, lemon is alkalizing to the body although it is acidic originally), this is also good for general detox
- Freshly juiced green vegetables (cucumber, kale, spinach, etc.), you may need to get a masticating (chewing) juicer (kind of looks like a meat mincing machine for vegetables and leaves) if you really like vegetable juices

If you can't commit to this, then try to have at least three alkalizing drinks a day. You can also broaden your scope of drink to some mineral/ spring water to which you've said 'Thank you' (or prayed) to repeatedly for a minute before drinking it. Research that stuff I mentioned back in chapter 2 about our vibration affecting the physical makeup of water crystals.

The ideal, in my opinion, is to thank every drink I have several times before drinking it; whether it's alkalizing spinach & cucumber juice, or an acidic cola. You can't go wrong with thanking the food and drink you consume, even if the effect is minute, it will add up over time with the amount of stuff we consume. I believe this is why saying 'Grace' (thank you prayer) before a meal aids in the digestion and nutrient absorption of that meal.

Whether chemically or spiritually, attack the quality of your water on all fronts!

Some would rather exorcise than exercise

I'd like to think that I'm a pretty muscular (ripped, jacked, chiselled) guy. One thing I noticed about exercise over the years is that consistency is far more important than how much you do in one session. I found that if you do 15-30 minutes a day (every day) of some light cardio, you will notice immense results in just two weeks; much more results than if you sat on your ass all week and binged with a huge 2 hour run.

My current regime consists of 15 minutes in the morning on my rebounder (mini trampoline) and 2-3 times a week of weight training. I don't take any protein/creatine/steroids to increase my gains, but I do have more green drinks and colloidal supplements on the weight training days.

Try it yourself! Commit to the following 2-week exercise regime and watch your levels of energy, health, looks, and wellbeing soar!

"Activity and sadness are incompatible."

- Christian Bovee

Movement, and the act of 'doing something' distracts and stimulates your mind, which will also make it impossible for you to fall into depression.

The two week consistently-getting-off-your-ass experiment

Observe and record your results if you want, and repeat the experiment as many times as required until desired results are achieved.

Normal day:

Do some stretches and about 15 minutes of low to mid-intensity cardiovascular exercise.

I recommend either on the mini-trampoline or an elliptical cross trainer. Simply because they are more efficient at working all your cells and are low-impact (I have an issue with my knee).

That's it; A couple minutes of stretching and a quarter of an hour of bouncing. I'm sure you can find time for this if you tried, no matter how busy you think your life currently is.

Weights day:

Still do your little morning routine, but throw in some resistance training. It's ideal to do this in the morning as well, however obviously you may have a job. In which case, go to the gym or do your weights at home right after work and **before** dinner. It may seem obvious, but don't do a workout right after a meal.

Your weights session should last between 30-45 minutes; of course you can do a little bit more if you want to, but don't do too much as this could result in tons of lactic acid building up in your muscles.

I find what works for me is focusing on a particular muscle group in any single weights session. I tend to get the best gains, and I'm not sore all over the next day, just in one area. I group them in the following way:

- Arms (shoulders, biceps, triceps, forearms, fingers?)
- Legs (quadriceps, calves, feet)
- Upper core (neck, chest [which you may also link with arms if you wish], upper back, upper sides)
- Lower core (abs, lower sides, bum)

I'm not going to get into the hundreds of different exercises you can do in each of these areas, do your own research. The internet has many great sources from respected publications that will help you make a workout plan for yourself, usually free of charge if you look hard enough.

In your session, I expect you will want to do several exercises, several times each. A general rule of thumb you should note is that if you're looking to build *more muscle*, then do low repetitions with high weight, if you want to build *strength* in the muscle you have do the opposite. For example:

More muscles	Strengthen existing muscles
3 sets of 10 reps with a weight with which you're struggling to actually do 10, 8, and 7 reps respectively.	**5 sets of 20 reps with a weight with which you're comfortable doing 20, 20, 20, 18, and 16 reps respectively.**
This means your muscles are actually being torn and strained (a good thing) and will rebuild themselves to be bigger and with more fibres.	**This means your muscles are getting used to having to utilize their fibres more efficiently, resulting in more strength.**

If for whatever reason you miss a weights day, just take a normal day and make your next day the weights day. Remember; **don't give up if you screw up!** Simply, resume the consistency the next day.

Week1:

This is just an example of your first week; feel free to adjust it to what *feels* best for you. For instance, if you're like me and already have huge muscular legs and want to do your arms and upper core twice in one week, then do so. Do remember to alternate weights days and normal days, as your muscles need a bit of time to rebuild and heal.

For the sake of argument, let's say it starts on a Monday, although you can start this on any day.

Monday: Normal day

Tuesday: Weights day – Arms

Wednesday: Normal day

Thursday: Weights day – Lower core

Friday: Normal day

Saturday: Weights day – Upper core

Sunday: Normal day

Week 2:

Monday: Normal day

Tuesday: Weights day – Legs

Wednesday: Normal day

Thursday: Weights day – Lower core

Friday: Normal day

Saturday: Normal day

Sunday: Weights day – Arms

Obviously, if you're feeling quite zealous you can always increase the overall length of the experiment. Who knows, you could even incorporate this into your subconscious as a habit for the rest of your life. Imagine what you'd look and feel like after 6 months of this, or a year?

Remember also, that you should always A.L.O.A.F, so try this experiment in conjunction with some (or all) of the other experiments.

Give it to her/him good old sport!

You should realize the importance of sex to a romantic relationship by now. Since you're already having plenty of it, you are probably already feeling the positive impact on your physical health... So I guess you can stop reading this section and go have yourself some sex.

However, even if you're single you should still have plenty of sex for the sake of your health. And don't forget to stay protected if you ARE going to go out and be a bit slutty. I promise you that a condom will not decrease the health benefits you get from it.

A recent study at a U.S. university discovered that having sex just twice a week resulted in a 30 percent increase (versus people that didn't get laid at all) in immunoglobulin A; which are little fellows that bind to invading baddies and then call in the cavalry (immune system) to wipe them out.

Another study by a university in the U.K. discovered that men who had sex 3 or more times a week **cut their risk of heart attack and stroke in half!**

The National Cancer Institute (U.K.) surveyed **30,000** middle-aged men and found that the ones who averaged 21 ejaculations a month showed a **33 percent lower risk of prostate cancer** than those with 4 to 7 ejaculations a month. So guys; even if you're alone and have nobody to have sex with, go ahead and have that moment of self-gratification and feel good about how well you're taking care of your health. Ladies, since this also applies to you, rediscover your rabbit.

Endorphins are also strong pain killers, and sex makes your brain release a fair share of these.

Remember, you can't overdo it. Well, you can in one day (it gets sore after I've had about 8, 30-40-minute rounds in 8 hours, with just minutes in between to rest and replenish fluids), but your parts should heal rather quickly and you can start all over, maybe even the next day.

(And yes ladies, I CAN)

Sex is a very alkalizing activity and quite complimentary to the alkaline diet. So go on and attack his/her/their front(s) often! (or back, or side, however you want to do it at the time...either way, go and get yourself some sex) And I do say 'attack' in an affectionate way, make sure you get consent.

Cancer: A symptom of a global psychic illness

What exactly is this 'cancer' that has the whole world living in fear?

I believe, simply put, that it is a symptom of a global disease that is currently ravaging humanity. Going back to the 'scalar levels of consciousness', we see that cancer is simply a cell which disconnects from the overall system. These cells now need to seduce, traumatize, stress and eventually disconnect other cells from the system to join the cancer. Since the powers that be are spreading Fear throughout humanity, the occurrences of cancer are also increasing.

The best 'scientific' method we have of dealing with cancer is chemotherapy, which has, at best, a 3% success rate. That is a startling statistic, when you consider how widespread the cancer problem is.

Analogously, we can equate the cancerous cells to the criminals that plague our society. They are simply organisms, full of fear and disconnected from Love.

Do not be afraid. Don't let my casual tone deter you; I honestly believe that *not fearing* something is the best defence against it. If you are unfortunate enough to currently have cancer, do not despair: you can be healed, I've seen it happen. If you do not, but are worried about getting cancer: Stop worrying! You see, when we give something our emotions and energy, it perpetuates it. How prevalent is cancer now in the global consciousness? Everybody knows and fears it.

I personally believe; that if you have a healthy state of mind, if you surround yourself with and practice Love, you meditate, you contribute, and you give your physical body all the nutrients it needs then **it is impossible to get cancer**.

Consider this...

Every case of 'miraculous spontaneous remission' of cancer has one commonality. All of the patients that have experienced it all recall a similar account of *having a feeling of complete peace and being a part of a perfect Loving system*.

There are many different methods and procedures that these 'miraculous' patients have used to get to that point. Some of which include:

- Meditation Therapy, Praying
- Laughter Therapy
- Homeopathic Medicine

Whichever combination of diet and lifestyle changes you use, always incorporate a feeling of complete and overwhelming Love. Love will always conquer Fear, and through Love you can conquer any disease.

The look represents the feel

When you've sorted out your internal physical and mental health, it's time to do a bit of work on the external.

Let me first begin by saying that I don't agree with today's shallow and looks-based culture. Obviously, in an ideal world, trivial matters of aesthetics would be irrelevant. But since we're living in a far-from-ideal world, we have to accept the fact that there are still lots of people out there who will 'judge a book by its cover'. (This is good if they're judging this awesome book by its awesome cover; it means more people will read it and hopefully improve their lives.)

Like most of us out there, I have been programmed to be aware of my external appearance. I have become addicted to the lovely feeling I get when someone looks at me and smiles at me because I'm gorgeous that day. If I create smiles and good feelings in people around me, this could only be a good thing.

This is not to say that you have to be overly-self conscious all the time and fear not looking your best. Keep a balance, don't stress over it. One of the most attractive features I notice in a person is confidence. I don't like the prissy girls that stress and worry about one hair being out of place. However, I equally dislike those dirty hippie chicks that don't bathe or shave. There is a perfect middle ground.

The way I see it, one should approach external aesthetics in the following way: Put in a bit of effort to establish the base (eg. shower, shave, wash your clothes from time to time, dress sensibly, put on your deodorant, etc.) and then simply let your healthy lifestyle, mindset and attitude make you a great point of attraction.

Smile! How many 'pretty' people are walking around being perceived as actually 'ugly' because of their miserable faces? In my experience, a *lot*! If you truly believe that God didn't bless you with a gorgeous visage, then don't compound your curse! You can still get at least 90% of the attention from the opposite (or same) sex as a 'beautiful' person if you consistently look sincere and happy. There are many women in my past that managed to acquire my *attention* despite having some aesthetic deficiency. When I think back to how they made me see their true beauty (underneath their physical flaws), it always seems to through accenting all their non-physical assets. Their smile and positive outlook have a much stronger impact than how well their makeup was put on. There's more on circumstance manipulation to attract a person in the relationship chapter.

To the women who read a lot of glossy model magazines: Stop starving yourselves! I don't care what the so-called statistics say, 95% of my straight male friends agree with me: If you look anorexic, we'll only want to give you one thing; and it's not a wedding ring or even a night of lust, but simply a sandwich. It's disgusting, we don't care what the media says, go eat something!

I'm sorry if I seem insensitive to eating disorders, but I truly believe that they can all be overcome by simply (truly) accepting yourself. Be grateful you're not some hideous creature living alone in a hovel; then, when you've accepted the fact that you're beautiful and start loving yourself for who you are, you can build on that foundation.

I can speak from experience about this whole topic.

I used to be a chubby one during my childhood and adolescent years, it didn't bother me until I noticed all my chunky peers shedding their pounds and starting to look great. Within the course of the year, I lost 20kg and have maintained my new ideal weight (comfortably) for over 8 years now. If a lazy glutton like me can do it, so can you!

The accentuation of your true beauty experiment

For best results, attempt this experiment in parallel with one or more of the other health-type experiments.

This experiment is simple. For the next two weeks, commit to incorporating the following points (if not done so already) into your regular routine.

- Preened and groomed: Make sure you look tidy and maintained (pluck those eyebrows, file those nails, dye (shave) that hair, etc.)
- Smiley despite all odds: Maintain a positive demeanour at all times when in public, if you must frown or cry, go home to your room and do it. You may feel a bit wrong not venting your woes and frustrations in public, but remember that you are simply conducting an experiment.
- Enhance your attitude: Speak only pleasant things to people, reserve judgements, bite your tongue in contentious situations, and imagine a positive aura of Love emanating from you that everyone is instantly attracted to.
- Make up: Do it differently for the next two weeks. Not just a different shade, a completely different style. This may give you the feeling of having a new face, with which you're trying out this world. Obviously this one is only for the ladies or Goths. For non-makeup wearing men, try styling your beard and hair differently.

- Mind your body (language): Pay more attention for the next two weeks to the signals your body is giving off when you're interacting with people. You don't have to become obsessed with it, but a little conscious observation goes a long way. Try to portray yourself as confident, mimic the actions of anybody you know that embodies confidence. Research several confident people and you will see commonalities like: calmness in speech, tall straight posture, relaxed and positive body language, and the like.

After the two weeks, results should show an increase in self-esteem, an increase in feeling desired (wanted, loved, all that mushy *aww* type stuff), and even possibly some renewed-confidence-wild-and-crazy sex sessions.

"Everything has beauty, but not everyone sees it."

- Confucius

Avoid unnecessary toxicity, it's just common sense

Whether you buy into the whole alkaline diet/ lifestyle or not, you should be able to recognize that the simple act of avoiding pollutants in your life has to be beneficial.

You can take simple steps everyday to avoid the pollutants that you can see, and the deadlier ones that you can't. Make a conscious effort (within reason, living in a sterile environment is actually counter-productive) to avoid the following if possible:

- Acidic (junk, non-) foods
- High levels of mental stress and worry
- Prolonged physical strain and stress (e.g. anaerobic exercise for hours in a row, exhausting manual labour)
- Living in/working in/prolonged exposure to a high-smog, low-tree area
- Excessive time in front of a T.V./Computer monitor
- Making excessive cell (mobile) phone calls, or even keeping your cell phone close to your body at all times (put it on the table when you can)
- Prolonged or consistent exposure to negative or depressing people (yes, seems a bit cruel, but you owe it to yourself to either help them sort themselves out or leave them with their misery)

However, don't start stressing about avoiding every little pollutant, lest you create more toxicity from your negative emotions.

So even if you're not willing to accept/endure the whole alkalinity lifestyle shift, you can still make educated and 'conventionally' scientific changes to drastically improve your health. Even if you're a sceptic to this whole 'holistic' approach to health, you deserve to be in a peak condition, however you choose to achieve it.

And yes, I acknowledge that we have very good internal systems that help shift all the crap that accumulates in our bodies: liver, lungs, kidneys, lymph nodes, etc. However, is it not logical to assume that if we overwhelm any system consistently, it will decrease in efficiency? People nowadays tend to think that our body systems will take care of us, despite us *not* taking care of our bodies.

We trust that our organs are designed to take this kind of consistent stress. Despite having a longer lifespan now than any time in history, we currently have the most and most elaborate ways of stressing our bodies.

That is exactly what we're doing: Drinking to excess consistently, with the hope that the liver will always be there to bail us out. We're eating more and more crap, assuming that our digestive tract and colon are more than happy to deal with it all. We're smoking more and more toxins, trusting that our lungs and lymph nodes will constantly come to our rescue.

However, after several years of this kind of abuse, the body does what any living thing would do: It reaches breaking point and fails. Think of your body parts as your good friends, they will love and help you unconditionally, but everyone has their limit. So when they no longer have the energy or means to support you, you will only have your habitual conscious thoughts to blame. Remember it is never too late to change your ways and start living with the health and vitality you deserve to.

Stay happy and healthy!

Section 4 – Emotions: Those lovely and vile biochemical reactions

Emotion – noun:

-a conscious mental reaction (as anger or fear) subjectively experienced as strong feeling usually directed toward a specific object and typically accompanied by physiological and behavioural changes in the body

Introduction to your emotions...

What is an emotion or a feeling? We all have them (some more than others), but rarely take time to analyze and interpret them. Most of our feelings are meant as feedback mechanisms to our brain to let us know that everything is awesome, or that something needs to change. Some emotions, in certain contexts, are helpful. Some emotions are empowering in ANY circumstance. For example: Happiness. No matter what occurs externally, it is ALWAYS beneficial to be able to put oneself in a state of happiness. It allows you to stay calm and collected so that you can make a 'sober' decision, compared to letting the sadness/anger/frustration take over.

Sometimes, a little bit of anger or some hostile emotion is needed in order to produce a desired result. For example, when you need to confront a bully, your own demons, or protecting someone you love. This subconscious need for a particular 'negative' emotion to manifest for survival is exemplified all the time in nature: When even the kindest and gentlest mother (of any species, humans included) fears for the safety of her young, she will turn into the most ruthless, angry and mean creature at the drop of a hat in order to protect them. When the danger passes, she returns to her usual emotional state. It's not the emotions themselves that are good or bad as such, it is our habitual use (or misuse) of them that determines their benefit (or detriment) in our lives.

The ONLY way we can feel bad, is to put the wrong emotion in the wrong context. Let me try to clarify this a little.

When you feel FEAR when you're about to walk into the middle of a road, and your autonomic nervous system makes your body jump back, it is beneficial as it stops you from getting killed. It is only when you constantly feel FEAR when you're trying to do something productive or just live your life in peace and it's holding you back, is when it's a bad thing. For most of us, these disempowering emotions are where we dwell on a daily basis.

Consciously controlling common cranial crap...

So we've established what an emotion is, now let's get a bit more of a handle on all the usual, day-to-day negative (debilitating or disabling) ones that tend to creep into our lives.

Usually, if we work a 9 – 5 j.o.b. (just over broke) we constantly feel pressure and stress from managers and colleagues. Most of us take our jobs (and even careers) way too seriously. Because the system is designed in such a way, nearly all of us have to be plugged into the system in order to have the means for mere survival. This subconsciously creates a dependency within us on the company/ organization which employs (enslaves) us. The best way to control this common cause of stress is to simply stop caring so much. I'm not saying stop being professional or doing your job to the best of your abilities. However, stop being influenced by the stress which is often being passed around.

Your boss comes into the office yelling and cursing, "The board report is due!" You need to do a particular part of the report, but you cannot because another department has not provided you with the relevant data. At this point most of us succumb to stress and frustration, calling this lacklustre department and perpetuating our boss's bad attitude at them. "Why haven't you got the data ready yet?!?! Don't you know that the senior managers need this report now?!"

Round and round the circle of stress goes. Does this pattern seem familiar?

I would not let my boss's stress rub off on me, I would simply and calmly state that I will keep chasing the department to get us the data, but there is nothing we can currently do so he should stop stressing as well. Suffice it to say this does not make me the most popular employee, since I will not let any manager make me a venting ground for their frustrations. However, I am efficient and dedicated; so the disagreeable fact that I do not perpetuate stress and instead choose to transcend it is usually forgiven.

I guess all I can conclude about feeling stressed is, "Chill out, it's not that important to stress over".

Remember that your job is not <u>you</u>, your lifestyle is not <u>you</u>, and your negative emotions are not <u>you</u>. You are an infinite, divine spirit which happens to be experiencing this physical life; therefore, anything negative in this physical life should be taken with a pinch of salt. Try to look at your life from this perspective and suddenly you will realize that all the negative feelings we experience originate in our own human minds. But, what do you do when you feel like a 'lesser' human? What if you think you're simply not 'good enough' to look at life this way or deal with its stresses?

The feelings of inferiority, offence, shame or worthlessness are all common among humans nowadays. Most people also often fall victim to a 'put-down' or insult, where a person makes you feel *inferior*. All I will say on this topic is that YOU are BETTER than them. People that put others down habitually are mostly insecure themselves. It is their only source of temporary relief, to feel that they are better than someone else, whether or not it's at all justifiable.

I simply laugh off anytime this happens to me. I used to be really quick-witted (hopefully I can still hold my own) so I would search out scenarios where I could actually participate in a 'burn off' with someone to see who had the better insults. I have become much wiser and no longer rise to it. In my mind, I simply pity and try to understand the insulter, knowing that they are in a much darker place in their lives than I. Remember most of those with acid tongues are merely trying to draw attention away from their own failings, without caring about your feelings. If you are fully comfortable with who it is you are, then they will never have the power to faze you.

Remember your true potential and how awesome you are, and no negative emotion will ever have power over you. With practice, you will actually be able to consciously decide what you feel; nobody will ever have the strength to put you in a disempowering emotional state.

Those are just a couple examples of what negative emotions can be catalyzed within us by others; however the strongest debilitating emotion at the core of them all is fear. It is the root cause of nearly all negative emotions and manifestations of them. Let's take a minute and examine this common enemy in detail.

F.E.A.R – F&k Everything and Run!*

Fear is the most common negative emotion that holds us back from getting what we want. It is the most debilitating of all the negative emotions.

I made up a little chart of a few of the most common fears, and what one can do to overcome them.

Fear Type	Ways it manifests	What can help
Fear of Rejection	• Not taking certain actions (which you know are beneficial) because of the possibility that somebody else might think less of (or reject) us • Being hesitant or indecisive about important issues	• **Developing a 'so what, next please!' attitude** • **The fact that if you don't try at all, you will fail 100% of the time** • **Emotional Freedom Technique (research it)**
Fear of Failure	• Not taking that next (or extra) step towards your goals because of the possibility that it may not work out; and in turn making you feel like a failure • Worrying about confirming the correctness of all the 'Naysayers' that told you that that 'you're not good enough for that'	• **Doing it anyways** • **With every 'failure' you learn new life lessons which may help you in a completely different area of your life**

(Continued)

Fear Type	Ways it manifests	What can help
Fear of Success	• Not embarking on the awesome future you deserve • Worrying about denying the 'Naysayers' their satisfaction, and therefore creating resentment • Having to play down your achievements, so as not to cause jealousy and resentment among your peers/loved ones	• **Start seeing that you deserve success** • **Although you may alienate your closed-minded group of peers, you can take comfort that they will be naturally replaced by better people**
Fear of Flying	• Could stop you from travelling abroad therefore limiting you to a smaller world • Stops you from visiting those relatives that live in that lovely, sunny and calm part of the world	• **Valium, Alcohol and herbal sleep aids (not all at once though, remember moderation)** • **Going to one of those flight courses with a simulator and cockpit flight apparently helps a lot**

When you get to grips with your particular fears, you'll see a whole new world which will open up to you. Don't expect them all to just dissolve overnight either, your subconscious has developed dependencies on some of them and won't just 'unlearn' them instantly. Be prepared to exert some mental effort and put in some hours to eventually master your fears. The following experiment should help to start you off.

Interrupt your pattern of disempowering behaviour experiment

This is my take on an NLP (Neuro-linguistic programming) technique. Please consult a professional if you choose to apply NLP in your life on an ongoing basis.

Please research "Pattern Interruption" and "NLP", to get other techniques and methods. Use them to help you master your emotions by programming your physiology and subconscious mind. In my eyes, Tony (Anthony Robbins) and Joseph McClendon III have this mastered, so make sure to research all their work on the subject.

Do the following technique for the next 2 weeks, every day, 10-20 rounds per day.

Preparation: Choose a disempowering state of mind or emotion you want to get rid of. (E.g. feeling sorry for yourself, depression, being afraid of failing, indecisiveness, etc.) Perhaps choose a time in your life when you felt that emotion most intensely or had that particular state of mind predominantly. Remember it clearly and feel the disempowering state intensely. For the purpose of this experiment, we'll call this the 'bad state'

Now, do the same for the complete opposite (positive) of that bad state. We will call this your 'good state'. For example, if your bad state is *sadness* then your good state is amazing *joy/ happiness*. Again, visualize an event where you were the happiest, overjoyed person in the world. Feel the amazing happiness and joy coursing through your veins.

Interruption and Celebration Gestures: Now that you have your bad and good states, it's time to choose an interruption gesture and a celebration gesture. They both could be anything you want, as long as they are done with emotional intensity.

Some examples of an interruption gesture are:

- Pinching yourself hard and yelling 'sadness be gone!'
- Splashing water in your face

- Slapping yourself in the face and yelling 'cut it out!'
- Anything else that shakes up your physiology and shifts your focus

Some examples of a celebration gesture are:

- Raising your fist in the air and yelling 'I'm awesome!'
- Looking up in the sky with both arms up and cheering
- Making a fist or two and ferociously saying 'F*&K Yeah!'
- Anything else you want to use as a feel-good emotional anchor

One Round:
In the first round you stay in your bad state the longest, maybe for a whole minute or so. You can use a timer/clock to help you keep track of how long you're doing it. Each round after that, you decrease the bad state time by a few seconds, until the bad state time is just a couple seconds.

1) Close your eyes and go into your bad state for the corresponding time period
2) Do your interruption gesture and then shake your body out quickly

3) Quickly then go into your good state for a few seconds (this time remains constant)
4) Do your celebration gesture

That's it!

You have just done one round of pattern interruption. Repeat this round 10 times, gradually decreasing the amount of bad state time.

Do a set of 10-20 rounds every day, maybe a couple of times a day for the next two weeks. If done properly, you will soon realize that you simply can't get back into the bad state again.

For the purposes of this experiment, do this when you're feeling fine, so as to program it into your nervous system.

After the first week of repeating the technique, feel free to actually use it when you find yourself in your bad state. Using the previous example, do your sets when you're feeling happy. However if you do find yourself feeling sad in any situation, feel free to use this then.

Yes, it may seem silly to slap yourself in the face and yell something out in the middle of an office meeting, but your emotional freedom is well worth it.

Happiness: that elusive little bugger...

We must all agree by now, that THIS is the spice of life. The trick is not to just spend your whole life chasing it, but actually HAVING it for as much of your life as you can.

The wisest teachers from all around the world will always tell you that **it comes from within**. This is where your search should start. I believe that happiness, joy, ecstasy, excitement are all just manifestations of Love. You cannot be happy if you do not have Love in your life. I'm not talking about the 'love' of substances, circumstances, ideals or material objects. I'm talking about True Love (God, Creation, or Infinite Consciousness) that we are all connected to at a visceral level.

To me, happiness is a choice; the choice can always be made, but in some situations it is more difficult to make than others.

Let us not forget that all of the manifestations of happiness are just emotions, which we know by now we can greatly influence.

If there is a remedy when trouble strikes,
What reason is there for despondency?
And if there is no help for it,
What is the use of being sad?

So come what may, I'll never harm,
My cheery happiness of mind.
Depression never brings me what I want;
My virtue will be warped and marred by it.

-Buddhist sage Nagarjuna

Some events are beyond your control, but your interpretation never is

Stuff just happens. It happens all the time. No matter how good you are at focusing on the good, remember that there are still people focusing on the bad. This may not result in anything bad actually happening directly to you, but you may witness or hear about something horrible that's happened. This in turn may make you feel bad, and therefore your vibration will be lowered by this external event. I'm here to tell you that how you feel about anything is directly correlated to what you *choose* to think. Why do some people look at the same so-called negative event and instantly feel bad, and others are unaffected, and others still are actually inspired?

Well, the ones that instantly feel bad are most people. They simply instinctively respond to a particular stimulus that their subconscious has been programmed with. They feel they have no control over how their emotions manifest and at the best of times will only try to avoid events and circumstances which are negative; which we all should know is impossible. They fail to grasp their own God-given mental powers and their own infinite potential. I realize that I'm using the word 'they' when you may consider yourself one of them.

My intention is that my words will trigger a chain-reaction in your mind and will make you consider the possibility that maybe you don't give yourself enough credit. Hopefully your brain will make some important distinctions and belief-shifts; which, in turn, will mean that you don't have to spend your life in the mental pen (livestock kind) with the rest of the Sheeple. (Get it? People are starting to resemble Sheep in all aspects, maybe except the fleece)

The ones who are unaffected are probably sociopaths or have some other 'mental disorder' which makes them desensitized to the world. They could also be people who simply don't care about anything until it affects them personally; and when it does they simply accept it, because 'that's just life'. My good friend calls them 'standard issue humans'. The ones who seem to just be space-filler; and to whom I always feel like saying: 'If you don't actually care, then just kill yourself and stop being a drain on resources of 'actual' people on the planet'. I don't however, because I like to think I'm an aspiring nice guy ☺

"One person with a belief is equal to ninety-nine who have only interests."

\- John Stuart Mill

Last but definitely not least, we have: the inspired ones. The ones who I aspire to be more like each and every day. To have the ability to look at a 'negative' event, stop yourself consciously, ask different questions and make different assumptions than most, remind yourself that 'we can't see the forest for the tree' and that this [event] is just a necessity in the greater picture. It takes lots of training and a bit of time to master; I'm not there yet, but I'm well on my way.

Let's put this into perspective for a moment with a hypothetical (or maybe secretly drawing upon my own life experience) case study.

The Decision: An imaginary case study on choosing to live on the bright side of life

(*_Life of Brian_ whistling ensues*)

A manager at some office is tasked with doing something deemed unpleasant to most. Due to the recession, he is forced to lay off (make redundant) several administrator staff. Two of the employees are in the same financial situation: a crappy one. They are both given the same exact speech by the manager, same embellishments, same reasons, and the same lame attempt by the manager at cushioning the blow. Both employees are also relatively equal in looks, brains, charisma, skills and experience.

What happens to one of them afterwards, however, is the complete polar opposite of what happens to the other.

Employee 'A' ***chooses*** to let this event break him down. He falls into depression and for the next several weeks eats delivered pizza and ice cream while sitting around his living room in his underwear, watching daytime soap operas and talk shows. He gets angry and resentful of his old company; 'how can those bastards just let me go?' he thinks to himself. When he's not angry, he feels saddened and useless; after all, he must be worthless or crap at his job if they let him go.

Employee 'B' ***chooses*** to see this as a motivational 'kick in the bum'. He wastes no time; in a couple of days, he has an updated CV (Resume) and sends it out to many employers, agencies, and websites. He sees all of this as an opportunity to advance in his career and gain more valuable experience in another company. Of course, he still gets the feeling that maybe it was all his fault and has a moment of self doubt. However, he quickly shakes off that feeling and quickly reigns in his thoughts back to the 'temple of positive intention'. Within a week he has his first interview, unfortunately he doesn't get it. He now has a decision to make, to simply give up and line up at the benefit (welfare) office, or to shake off this perceived 'failure' and persevere.

He still ***chooses*** not to let this deter him; after all, to him this just means that he wasn't meant for this job and something even better is waiting just around the corner. The following week he gets two more interviews, he gets offered *both* jobs! He rejoices in how amazing this makes him feel, and ends up taking the one that *feels* best for him. Knowing that there is still an unfilled position in the job that he didn't take, he calls 'A' in case he didn't find a job yet.

Sure enough, a month after they lost their jobs, 'A' is still stuck in a rut and his little bit of savings is all but gone. 'B' informs him that there is probably still an opening at a particular office, since he had to turn it down as he accepted a different position. If he hurries, he might still be able to get it; 'B' even offers to recommend him to the company. 'A' is apprehensive and sceptical, but eventually reluctantly decides to send in his CV.

The position is still open, he's informed, and he secures an interview. 'A' turns up to the interview with his negative attitude; knowing that he needs the job, but constantly thinking 'I'm not good enough for this', 'I always blow it in interviews', and 'Stupid 'B' giving me his leftover scrap of a job that he didn't want'. He ***chooses*** to focus on all the negatives before the interview has even started.

What happens next? It should be obvious by now. Needless to say 'A' didn't end up getting the job, as he 'knew' he wouldn't anyway. He becomes resentful and jealous of 'B' and ends up breaking off all contact. The weeks, months and years roll on and his downward spiral continues. He continues his 'blame mentality' and points his finger all around at the alleged causes of his misery. Eventually, when his situation deteriorates to the point where he can't afford rent, his subconscious kicks into action. However, since both his subconscious and conscious minds are convinced that he doesn't or shouldn't get anything amazing in his life, it finds him just enough resources to survive. He manages to secure an assistant supervisor position at a local fast food joint, making just enough to pay the bills and fund a newly-developed food and alcohol addiction. The rest of his life is to be a descent into mediocrity.

Conversely, 'B' is doing amazingly at his new job. He has had two promotions since then and his money worries are a thing of the past. He faces all new challenges at work now, but because of his awesome attitude, he considers them fun challenges which allow him to grow and develop, and not 'problems' which he must battle with and overcome. All of his other areas in life are also awesome. He's developed a relationship with a beautiful woman (who actually isn't with him for the money, although he's certainly got enough of that now), he's toned and healthy and goes to the gym a couple of times a week, and most importantly: He's happy!

A couple of years later, 'B' takes his office team of employees (that he's now managing) out for a fast-food lunch. He's well-off now, so decides to win favour with his subordinates by paying for everyone's food.

It just so happens, that 'A' is working at this particular joint. He has really let himself go in just a couple years: he's obese, he hates his job (still assistant supervisor), all of his friends have gradually distanced themselves from him, he's miserable, and the only thing staving off suicide is looking forward to the temporary pleasure of stuffing his face with food and alcohol when he gets home.

Both men, started out in the same place, with the same resources, in the same circumstances were now at opposite ends of the spectrum. 'A' and 'B' now look at each other over the fast-food counter, recognize each other and both think: **'How the hell did you end up there?'**

The answer to their question is simple: Choice. They each **chose** to interpret events that 'happened' to them in a different way. One is clearly empowering and helpful, the other is clearly not.

"Everything can be taken from a man or a woman but one thing: the last of human freedoms, to choose one's attitude in any given set of circumstances, to choose one's own way."

- Viktor E. Frankl

This story is obviously a hypothetical exaggeration, but I see things 'like' this happening all around me almost every single day. Don't be like that loser; ***choose*** to feel good in any circumstance. Choose to be awesome!

The response interjection experiment

Try this conscious technique for the next two weeks.

First, decide consciously that you will stop yourself every time something 'negative' or displeasing happens to you.

Every time this happens, make up a new and positive interpretation of said event or circumstance. Especially when your brain yells out, 'There is no alternative meaning, it's just bad!'

Remember you get the most growth in any area when you exercise your will in the most difficult times.

For example:

Seemingly negative minor event	New and positive potential interpretations and benefits
You miss the bus	• Now you can get some fresh air and exercise while you walk to your destination • You have an excuse why you're late • You don't have to smell that horrible, old crack-head that sits in the back • You've just saved (and therefore '*earned*' according old Ben Franklin) a dollar or two!
You overcook a meal	• You've just learned how long NOT to leave that particular thing on the fire • You've gained experience that will make you a better chef in future
Someone offends/ insults you	• Make you consider that maybe, just maybe you may be too uptight as you actually let someone injure you with words • Don't draw attention to it, because the other person is obviously lashing out because of personal pain • You can disregard it and laugh at them (sometimes makes them angrier, hehe) • Whatever they said isn't true anyway, you can retaliate with a more honest and wittier retort; maybe even make them apologize and think about their own actions more

(Continued)

Seemingly negative minor event	New and positive potential interpretations and benefits *(Continued)*
Someone cons/scams/ steals from you	• **They obviously needed it more than you; in a way you've just been indirectly (if involuntarily) generous, good karma points for you** • **They won't find happiness this way, thieving bastards!** • **You have an excuse to replace your old item with a better one** • **You can report them to authorities, and do your bit in stopping more people in getting done over by that person** • **It's a chance to send out the vibration of 'I am abundant and whatever I lose will be replaced or reimbursed tenfold'**

"Easier said than done", you may be saying to yourself after reading that list. Trust me, it seems that way at first, but after a while it can become an easy habit. It took me just two short weeks to become proficient and now do it unconsciously when faced with any difficulty.

And some big ones which I wouldn't wish on anyone:

Major event traumatic	New and positive potential interpretations
You get sacked (fired)	• Opportunity to find a better job • No regrets about leaving your current employer • You're better than that place anyway • You don't necessarily have to get up early for a while • You can get severance (redundancy) pay • Sympathy and support from close ones
A loved one dies	• Now they can live on forever in your memories, however you choose to remember them • They can scope out heaven ahead of time for you and bring you up to speed when you get there • May sound a bit cruel ,but, your worries about their health and/or welfare are now over • They are free from the confines and troubles of this world
You're diagnosed with an 'illness' that is currently believed to be terminal	• Modern technology is quite advanced and can perform miracles • There are people now who have been 'cured' of every 'disease' that exists • It gives you time to reflect and consider what things in life are actually important

(Continued)

Major event traumatic	New and positive potential interpretations
	• **Whatever doesn't kill you can only make you stronger, so *when* you get cured you will have built character and resolve** • **Diseases aren't the cause of bacteria or viruses, so all you need to do is get rid of all the toxins in your blood and mindset and the disease will dissolve away 'magically'** • **Your work on this planet is far from done, therefore you will NOT let some f&%king condition interfere with your work** • **Lots of sympathy, attention and understanding from loved ones or work people; which should make your day-to-day life a little easier** • **You can probably get some legal, medicinal marijuana for your condition; so if you must part with this world, you can do it while being high off your face**

It's not whether the new chosen interpretation is fully believable or not, it's all about how it makes you feel. Try to enhance and embellish all the already positive events whenever you can and, at least, try to decrease the negativity of 'bad' events. And obviously, wherever possible, turn a seeming negative all the way around into a positive.

Remember also, that you should always A.L.O.A.F, so try this experiment in conjunction with some (or all) of the other experiments.

Section 5 – On Relationships

Is the hermit/loner alone because he's miserable or miserable because he's alone?

One might say that is like asking which came first, the chicken or the egg. It doesn't really matter; suffice it to say that we all need some form of relationship in our lives to stay happy and healthy. Obviously this means that if we're to even remain sane we must have some sort of 'company' from time to time. Even recluse hermits develop relationships with the animals/objects in their home because their subconscious needs it. Remember the movie 'Castaway'?

(A castaway (Tom Hanks) makes a friend out of a volleyball to keep himself company.)

Anyone we continually interact and communicate with is someone with whom we have a relationship.

We're not going to get along perfectly with everyone in our lives all the time. That's just a fact. All we can do is master the relationship Front of our lives and aim to have great relationships with most of our people, most of the time.

How do we end up moving away from people in the first place? How and why do relationships break down in the first place? It's all subjective. When we blame the other person and not look within for the true answer, we will constantly see fault in everyone around us.

From your own point of view, it could blatantly be someone else's fault that things aren't working between you. However, this could mean you should yourself change your interpretation of events, or it could simply mean that your vibration level is too far away from this person's to currently have a relationship with them. Don't be saddened by this, sometimes it's just the wrong person or the wrong time or both.

So now that we've established that relationships are here to stay, let's look at improving and polishing the relationships in our lives.

Develop or degenerate; stagnation is an illusion

You can see this exemplified greatly in the area of relationships. Whether it's the relationship with yourself, your partner, your friend or your family member, if you don't cultivate it, it's actually suffering. If you don't make some progress in any relationship for a certain period of time, you can notice that the relationship has suffered. There is no such thing as stagnation in a relationship. If you've been in a 'not great, but not horrible' romantic relationship for example, you will notice that after a while you start losing interest in that person, you stop enjoying the same things and you start to forget what it was that drew you to them in the first place.

Even the good friends that I haven't seen for a couple of years due to travelling are going to be different from the people that I knew then. I am aware that I will have to get to know them all over again. Dependant on the strength of the original rapport and how I left things will determine the length of time that this *re-bonding* will take. I still have old good friends who I only manage to see every couple of years, with whom re-establishing the connection is still instant. We just catch up on the latest events in each other's lives and try to momentarily live those events instantly through each other's eyes.

Before we get ahead ourselves and start discussing interactions with others, let's get reacquainted with our own selves first.

You don't have to be schizophrenic to have a relationship with yourself

How do you cope with who you are? In your mind, do you praise yourself or put yourself down? What are your feelings towards your *current* identity?

We all have a relationship with ourselves, whether we are aware of it or not. We all know that we are able to be our own worst critic, but we should not forget that we can also be our own #1 fan. Too much of either can be detrimental, so make sure to balance the part that holds you to an ever-increasing standard and the part that just cheers you on regardless of success.

There is a subtle distinction between arrogance and self-appreciation. Despite what our parents might have told us, it is NOT wrong to be proud of ourselves. Obviously we step into the arrogant realm when we start believing that our **egos** are the be-all and end-all. If you are able to abstract yourself from your own subjective physical experience and thank your strong connection with the Infinite Consciousness that you are able to experience everything in life that you do, then you stand a good chance of having a confident and strong relationship with yourself.

I am sometimes (okay, often) mistaken for being a bit up my own ass, because I don't always take the time to explain myself. I feel that since I have 'God' (Infinite Love, True Self) and not my ego to thank for everything I am and have, then I should be grateful for my connection and express it accordingly. To quell the pride of using God-bestowed potential is silly.

But I digress...

You can be proud of who you are without being condescending or smug about it. If you live to the best of your abilities and are less humble about it in your head, you will be able to achieve even more and be able to give more to others. One funny thing I noticed is that *people won't resent your success or happiness if it ends up helping them as well.*

Be careful not to get carried away with feelings of superiority: Yes, it's okay to advertise how awesome you are; No, it's not okay to hold it over someone else. Make sure that whenever you brag to someone about your achievements, that you also mention the ways they could also have similar achievements if they so wished.

Don't be afraid to be happy with who you are, you deserve to be. If people get offended by your expressions of happiness, then feel sad for them for they could not feel as such, if they were happy themselves.

Acquaintances, friends and good (closest) friends

Some people don't even make the distinction. If you consider everyone you have a conversation with, a good friend, then you open yourself up for disappointment and potentially betrayal. On the other end of the spectrum, if you've known and met with someone consistently for several years and only consider them an acquaintance, then you're obviously too closed-off and won't get all the benefits that close friendships have to offer.

Not to say that everyone you know fits nicely into one of these categories. Some of your people may be in between categories.

Your mind may promote or demote people according to their merits. For example, if someone constantly lets you down or causes you to feel bad about yourself, your mind may eventually move them into a 'lower-connection' category or completely end the relationship.

Acquaintances are people you have a positive inclination towards, but don't necessarily trust or like enough to constantly stay in contact with.

Friends are people with whom you have some things in common, but may not trust enough to know your most intimate secrets.

Your good friends are the people who you actually trust, whose company you enjoy, and around who you can be the 'real' YOU. (We all, at some point have to put on an act; like pretending to be a model employee at an interview, or being nice to your girlfriend even though she's being a bitch for no reason.)

Blood Ties

Yup, blood is thicker than bread and water. The thing about family is that for good or ill, you're literally born into it.

I happen to be blessed with possibly the best parents in the world. They love me and my little brother unconditionally and have sacrificed so much to give us a good start in life. I have an awesome little brother who I have a great relationship with and with whom I can talk about things that I wouldn't with anyone else in the world (including the Trouble & Strife [Cockney rhyming slang for: Wife]). I have a couple of close cousins back in the Old Country and some very nice aunts, uncles, great aunts, etc.

For the most part, I have an awesome immediate and extended family. However my Dad's side is completely horrid. His mother, siblings and their offspring are some of the worst examples of humans around. I'm not going to air my historical dirty laundry here, suffice it to say they've done so much harm to both my parents that I've effectively disowned them all. I know I shouldn't really feel this strongly about people who I now have practically no contact with, but that's the thing about family. I suppose I dislike them so, because I hate the fact that I'm related to them. Oh well, I digress. The point I'm trying to make is that nobody's family that I know is perfect. You will always have some members who you will get along with, and others that you won't.

'The one', 'The only', 'The other half', 'The ball and chain', 'The Love of your life'

That one in your life with whom you should be able to share anything. The one who helps you make your life the easiest and most difficult. That lovely person that makes the sun come up. You know the one; the one for whom you'd do anything. She/he makes live worth living.

I'm talking of course about your current romantic relationship. This is the place where you can go to cultivate your truest loving emotions and give your all to another consciousness.

When you find a person that meets the vibration level of your soul, everything flows naturally and correctly. You don't have to remember all the tips you learned in the self-help relationship books you read. Everything seems to fall into place on its own.

However, when the honeymoon period is over, there must be more present than the initial 'loved-up' feeling for your relationship to endure. Mainly, the Principles of Attraction are the key in maintaining happiness within a relationship. I have personally used them (along with the mind-hacking experiments, Section 2) to attract the woman of my dreams. I am still using them to keep my relationship fresh, exciting and full of Love.

Just like with friends, this main life relationship must be 'maintained' in a sense to keep it growing and stop it from stagnating. (Actually degenerating, as mentioned earlier.)

As my Mom always says:

"A relationship is like a flower, you must nurture and take care of it, lest it die"

How do you know if you're currently with (or still stalking) your 'the one'? Well that's one I'll have to leave you to figure out for yourself. Only you can form your own conscious and subconscious criteria that will attract your soul mate.

If you're unsure if a particular individual is worth entwining your soul with, you can ask a few simple questions:

- Can I physically spend long amounts of time with this person? Do we enjoy each other's company?
- Do I easily visualise an awesome life with this person in five (ten, twenty or fifty) years?
- Are there any huge belief contrasts on fundamental issues?

Remember, even if you answer 'Yes' to a million of questions like this but it still 'feels' wrong, then make sure to always listen to your heart before your head in these matters. Then again, that might just be the suppressed romantic in me talking.

Now, if I haven't been sappy enough in this section, allow me drizzle a little more honey from the pot. Here's a story I hope you will enjoy.

The English Rose and the Canadian Weed

Once upon a spring, there was a beautiful English Rose. The Rose was starting a new job in a new garden. Full of life and optimism, she entered the greenhouse in which she would be working. There was nobody else in that greenhouse except a rather scruffy looking Weed. The Rose, with her sunny disposition, optimistically introduced herself to the Weed. The Weed was left breathless, that is, he was temporarily unable to photosynthesize.

The Weed was instantly smitten with the beautiful Rose. The Weed tried to play down his shabby appearance by explaining that *all plants* were like this in Canada.

They spent their days working in the same greenhouse, doing their own respective duties.

Several weeks after, two Nettles moved into the greenhouse, one was quite thin for a Nettle; the other was huge, even for a Pumpkin, never mind a Nettle. Although the Nettles sat in the same greenhouse, they were hardly noticed by The Rose or The Weed. By this point, the Rose and Weed were completely captivated with each other. The two of them went on working in the same greenhouse for some weeks after that. The Weed would not let The Rose know how he truly felt, so as not to jinx his chances. He then decided that she would be his Forever.

There was only one problem: The Rose, outside working hours, was with a Rice Plant. That, in itself, would not have been such a problem, but this particular Rice Plant had a great inheritance of a monetary nature. The Rose would go to the Rice Plant's huge garden on the weekends and swim in his pool. The Rose seemed to have a lifestyle deserving of her grace and sophistication.

The Weed however, was convinced that The Rose was not truly happy. He saw the expression on her petals; he knew she was more than she gave herself credit for. This is the only thing that gave him hope. Even if nobody else could sway The Rose from her Rice Plant for the years she was with him, The Canadian Weed decided he would make her petal's glow and blossom in a way no other plant could. If only she knew how he truly felt.

He began to brag about all the shrubs and daffodils he'd been with and how much he was enjoying not having a steady flower of his own. He did this to see if The Rose actually had any real feelings for him. All this did was make The Rose think that The Weed was only out to sow his seed. He had all but given up hope and started to doubt if he actually could make her truly happy.

Then one fateful day, The Weed wrote The Rose a long letter on one of his leaves. He let her know everything he felt; and that he understood that he was a scruffy Weed and she was a beautiful and sophisticated Rose, and that's why it would never work. The Weed was just making himself feel better about how he failed to woo her. However, it was those words that made The Rose think, and realize that she actually felt something for this scruffy Weed.

After many weeks of courting and solidifying intentions, The Rose finally left the Rice Plant for The Canadian Weed. Then, by her love and grace; the previously scruffy weed turned into an awesome Amaranth. He became such an incredible and amazing plant; with bright colours and majestically flowing leaves. He didn't even realize what true happiness was until that day.

The Rose and The Amaranth bought themselves a lovely plot in the most exclusive garden, in the most expensive park in the whole country. Neither of them had known such intense Love before and they were both truly happy. They've had many wonderful experiences since then and helped make the world a better place.

Needless to say, they are living happily ever after.

The End

(The preceding is based on a True Story)

So you see, even if you think you're a scruffy-looking weed, you should still try for the beautiful rose. At the very least, to make her appreciate her own beauty; but also, through her love, you may realize you're more than the scruffy-looking weed you give yourself credit for.

The art of attracting a member of the opposite sex

I hope you gathered from the previous story, that there are no 'leagues' of people which indicate who you can attract. It is a social construct that keeps like breeding with superficial like. It maintains the status quo, by limiting people's range of attraction to within their perceived 'peer' group.

Remember, it doesn't matter if you think that he/she is too rich/tall/pretty/smart/cultured, he/she *is within your grasp* if you just believe it. 'Leagues' are just imaginary boundaries that exist in most people's minds that prevent us from even trying. Once you shift your mindset to 'I can attract anyone I truly want', you will actually be able to.

Whether you want to find and attract a Keeper, a bit of fun, a Sugar Mommy/Daddy, or a dirty little secret; the rules on initial attraction are pretty much all the same. Obviously you're going to steer things into their own categories after the initial ice-breaking (able to hold conversations with each other) has occurred and mutual attraction established.

Unfortunately, I do not know anything substantial about same-sex interactions. I suppose I could've asked some of my gay and lesbian friends to shed some light, but that would be cheating. In this chapter, I only want to draw upon my own personal experiences, and although I have attracted the odd homosexual man and woman in my day, I did it inadvertently by being a very desirable (and modest) guy (☺). The next part may be useless to you if you are homosexual, so I advise you to get a book on physical attraction for your particular orientation. However, some of the things may still apply to you, so use at your own discretion.

I must warn you, the next two sections on targeted attraction may de-mystify some of the aspects around flirtation and initial interactions with an object of your desire. Some of the advice may also seem a bit devious or cruel. I'm just trying to give you some options; when your mind (or desperation) makes you start trying what you deem to be *manipulative* instead of *fair strategy* is up to you. Keep in mind also, that these are just my opinions and have only a 90-95% success rate. Remember, there are always people/timings/ circumstances/ mindsets which will not be compatible with the following strategies. So please don't hold me responsible if you get a telling-off or a drink-in- the-face from saying/doing something I inspired you to do.

Conversely, if through something I mention you happen to find your soul mate or become the successful 'player' you wish to be, then do feel free to thank me. I am a praise-junkie and let me take this time to give you a cheeky pre-emptive 'You're welcome'.

Please remember though, that no matter what strategy or approach you use to 'get' them, it is only the true you that will determine whether you keep or lose them.

The following section should be used with caution and earnest consideration.

For women: how to attract any man (or realize he's not actually worth attracting)

- Flaunt it if you got it

Even if you don't 'got it', flaunt it anyways. Make sure the object of your desire is looking at you when you do. The amount of aesthetically-deficient females that I found sexy because of a certain skirt or some extra skin showing is quite high, but that's just me.

See the *accentuation of true beauty experiment* in section 3 for more advice on this.

- Stroke his ego before you stroke anything else.

The amount of women that 'got' me in the past simply because they catered to my intellectual (or otherwise) vanity is daunting. Don't overdo it, but act impressed with almost every stupid thing he brags about. A guy will choose an ego stroke over a hard-to-impress girl any day of the week. We're simple creatures... but you women already know that.

- Let him be (or think he is) in control

No matter how submissive, passive, or laid back the man is, he will need the sense of having some control at some level. If he thinks he's in the driver's seat, he's definitely more likely to give you a ride. (Metaphorically and literally)

- Feign interest in his hobby, not his passion

If you're going to attempt to bond using a common activity, make sure it's just his pastime and not his true passion. Men are very territorial about their passionate interests and do not want women encroaching on their domain. We will, however, like having fun activities in common with our women.

Those are just a couple of hints for women out there who want to win the affections of a man.

There are fewer things women need to do to get men, then vice versa. This is simply because men are simpler creatures, well most of them anyways. Sorry boys, but you know I'm right. Let's put it this way, if we were as complicated as women, we might actually stand a chance of understanding what goes on inside their heads.

We may be simpler to figure out, but have (on average) less stress in our lives. So it is a trade-off, and no gender is 'better'.

For men: how to attract any woman (or realize she's not actually worth attracting)

- Very carefully act like you don't even want her attention

When executed properly, is the easiest way to win a woman's attention (potentially more). This must be done with the utmost tact and moderation. Don't blatantly ignore obvious advances, but make her aware of your indifference whenever she's prancing around looking for your attention/ approval.

- An oldie but a goodie: Pretend to (or actually convince yourself to) care about her passion

Find out what she loves more than anything in the world, and research the hell out of it. Make sure to instantly say that you are also into whatever it is the first time she mentions it. Most of the time you can also get away with just generically saying something like 'I've always been interested in X, but never had time to really get into it, maybe I should try it sometime'.

Possibly followed on with an 'I suppose I would need someone to guide me on X, hmmm... do you know anyone that could be a source of good info?'

If you're lucky and she's eager to share her passion, you're 'in there' under the guise of the common interest. Who knows, even if you didn't previously care about whatever it is beforehand, you may have found a great new interest.

Conversely, you may find that she's into things that bore you to death; at this point you can re-evaluate your initial attraction as you saw her from a different angle.

- Accentuate your ability to protect or to entertain

At any point in a woman's life she'll be dominantly searching for either someone to protect/defend or to stimulate/excite her. You have to do some 'listening' first to ascertain which of these two the woman is looking for at this particular time. Then, simply exaggerate how rich/stable/strong/secure/ powerful or how wild/exciting/crazy/funny/ entertaining you are. If you're (un)lucky enough to choose a woman who is constantly switching between the two, you're going to have to work harder and synchronize your boasts with her feelings.

Remember, Gold-diggers are simply insecure women who think that they couldn't possibly fend for themselves in the cruel world, although they very resourcefully do a great job of separating you and your cash.

- Make her feel special (whether you found your 'the one' or you just want a lay)

I found that this need is far stronger in women than men. For example, at a party once I said something about the insignificance of our planet in relation to the size of the universe. Instantly a debate sparked and the teams were formed in a matter of seconds. All the men were mostly fine with this notion, but the women kept arguing how 'special' and 'blessed' we all were to be alive and here now. This was just an isolated incident, but seems to be conducive to the theory that women simply need to 'feel special' more than men.

So obviously there are countless ways to 'exploit this potential security breach' and slip by the *inhibition and apprehension guards* that defend her fortress of affection. However, whatever methods you use, always have in mind this one end result:

She subconsciously associates YOU with her main source of feeling special and happy.

Once this is achieved, you are 'in there'!

When you are, you have a duty to be considerate. If you're just using her for some fun, make sure she understands that's all there is. Nothing disgusts me more than guys who string girls along for ages with no intention of committing. Make sure you always understand the status of all your relationships, whether they last a night or many years.

Symbiotic and Parasitic Mutual Influence

Do you have people in your life which you know are a good influence on you? I hope so. Take a moment to just categorize everyone with whom you spend time on a regular basis into three simple groups:

A) I feel good/inspired/motivated/excited being around them

B) I feel neutral/indifferent/detached being around them

C) I feel bad/depressed/offended/upset being around them

Now count the amount of people in each category. The ratio I am now always aiming for is:

Category A: 80%

Category B: 15%

Category C: 5%

Obviously this means that you should mostly have positive influences surrounding you whenever it's possible. Make sure that these people genuinely wish you well in all circumstances, not the types that are only happy as long as you're NOT. This Symbiotic group is made up of people that you can help, and that also help you; everyone benefits from the relationship and you're both enriched from the interactions.

A couple of indifferent/neutral people are needed to provide contrast between 'freaking awesome' and 'just okay' types of mindsets. Sadly I think most of the planet falls into this category, but remember it's subjective. The people who I deem have a neutral influence on me, might actually be beneficial to those who are in a much darker place. They may also be 'not positive enough' for some enlightenment-obsessed hippies.

Lastly, we should have nearly no negative influences in our lives. It's okay if we keep that one old grumpy man/woman, as they will give us the most observational contrast between where we are and where we *never want to be.*

Do you have someone in your life that makes you lose the will to live when you're around them?

I do, I have an aunt in Poland who is the biggest 'Skrobi Dupa' (which literally translates into *ass-scraper*) I've ever met. This term alludes to someone who would literally scrape the faeces off their posterior and ingest it to save some money on their grocery bill. She's one of these 'standard issue humans' that sludge through life, not knowing or searching for happiness, but striving to make everyone else's life a misery while complaining about how horrible life is. The kind of person that denies her own family financial aid because 'times are hard' while secretly stashing away cash under her mattress, God knows for what. Surely if you or your family is in dire need, THIS is what the secret funds would be for. These are the kind of people that are true evil in the world. Sure, some may argue that an armed robber would be much worse. But at least, he's honest that he's robbing you, and once it's over, it's over.

These low-vibration, ill-intentioned, hate and resentment harbouring degenerates will grind on the positivity and resolve of their surroundings until there is no energy for them to feed off of. They are trapped in a downward spiral and are dragging down anyone they can latch onto.

Keep in mind though, that I do not hate her, I simply pity her. I am not harbouring some grudge, where the disgust and ill-feelings grow more powerful every day. I have simply chosen to limit physical contact with her, and have put her in the far recesses of my mind. No ill will, No resentment, No revenge... simply put: No Attention.

Enough experiences with these people have taught me, that whoever I must be around out of obligation to friends/family/society has to still be at a certain vibration level. I'm not saying that it's easy to stop being around someone completely if there are some obligations which force you to interact, but a certain detachment must occur to avoid being brought down to their level. Remember this isn't being snobby or judgmental about the type of person you associate with, but one must be a tad discerning. (As my monocle falls into my brandy glass.)

That's the way it seems to work with these miserable bastards, they don't want to hear about how to get up to where you are, they want to tell you why you're not actually (or shouldn't be) as happy/successful/healthy/lovely/cute/etc. that you think you are. The only satisfaction they get is from knowing that they somehow dragged you down closer to their level. Unless you are strong enough to raise them out of these ingrained destructive patterns of thinking, you will be the one suffering at their hand. Save them if you can, but if you can't then move on; remember that mutual subconscious influence between people is constantly happening.

Here's a good rule of thumb to use on whether or not someone in your life has reached the point where you're considering to distance yourself from or purge them completely: Ask yourself how many times this person has made you happy recently, how many times they made you smile; conversely: how many times they brought you down, how many times have they made you doubt yourself, how many times they made you feel negative emotions. Now put the numbers of positives as a percentage of the total. My minimum number is 10% positive; meaning that if they make you feel like shit 90% of the time or more, maybe it's time to evaluate the amount of contact with said person.

That's not to say you can't be more harsh or discerning if you choose. Some people I know have a 50% threshold. (i.e. if a person doesn't make them happy or is enjoyable to be around at least half of the time, they phase them out of their lives)

Remember to *Attack the Relationship Front* from the subconscious programming angle as well. Use the mind hacking experiment from Section 2 to form beliefs like 'everyone in my life loves me' and 'I benefit everyone that I come into contact with'.

Section 6 – Money: Doesn't buy happiness, but is essential to its facilitation

All about mindset

I'm not going to get into my views about whether money and capitalism are good ideas or not. I could write pages and pages arguing For and Against, but it would be to no avail.

Money is here to stay, at least for a couple of generations; until the world reaches enlightenment and everyone is rich and happy, and poverty is a thing of the past. So with that out of the way, let's focus on how to get you more digits (in the +) in your bank account. Even if the destruction of all our monetary systems is imminent due to natural cataclysms or global wars, you should still make some money to buy supplies for the 'transition period'.

As the title of this section would suggest, having or lacking money is all about mindset. It wasn't until I realized this and stopped stressing about 'not having enough' that I started to be financially secure. I kept repeating consciously to myself that money is abundant in the world and it is constantly flowing towards me from many sources. I concurrently started the mind-hacking experiment (back in chapter 2, if you've skipped ahead to here) focusing on my first 10,000 dollars of pure extra profit. Not having a 10k bonus to my salary, having **all** of it after tax, and separate from my work salary. In that year, I made 10,030 dollars after tax. Obviously this concreted my faith in this new-found power, and I've been practicing this life ideology without any scepticism ever since.

Whatever your current financial and employment situation is, if it's not ideal, then it **is** improvable. You must come to terms with the fact that it is possible for you to be financially independent. How quickly it ends up physically happening is directly correlated to the intensity of your belief and willingness to simply accept the fact that you are already rich.

So what does this mean? What should you start doing or thinking about?

Focus on your imminent wealth, not eliminating your debts

This may seem like a subtle distinction to make, but trust me its ramifications will be immense.

I've said it before; it's all in your mindset. If you're constantly focusing on making enough money to meet all your financial obligations, then that is the best you can hope for. That is the absolute maximum to which your subconscious will seek out and acquire funds. Does it not then make more sense to focus on having enough money to live your dreams? Since at the very least, that number will be much higher than simply paying off your current debts.

To put it another way, if you were to correlate your net worth directly to your happiness and you were at – 20,000 happiness points; would it not make more sense to focus on +100,000 instead of 0? Even if we assume that we will always land somewhere between here and our ideal goal, it is better to shoot for the stars; because ending up just below the stars is far better than actually achieving the two stairs up that you hoped for. Simply put; the bigger your dreams are, the greater your reality will be.

Use all of your subconscious programming techniques as well, in order to get the universe to start amassing your future wealth. Most importantly, you must decide to be rich, and start living accordingly.

If they can do it, why can't I?

That's the most inspiring question I ever asked myself which made me believe it's possible to achieve anything. Look at some of the most business-successful people in the world today; let's face it, they're not necessarily the brightest stars in the sky. I see geniuses living in poverty every day, and I think to myself: what a waste of potential. Then I see love-starved, ungrateful, uninspired, little men with anger issues yelling at people on national television that the business world is cruel and that YOU have to be as cruel to succeed in it. Not to mention all their 'yes-men' who kiss their asses so hard you'd think they came down with a case of Resistant Swine Flu and that this 'tycoon's' ass had the antidote inside. So much more reverence and respect is given to these 'gurus of the business world' than is deserved. It is no great feat to dedicate your life solely to the material.

In my belief, it is only natural, that if I woke up with 100 Million tomorrow, I would give away at least 50 Million in the next couple of weeks. I think a lot of people forget that 'YOU CAN'T TAKE IT WITH YOU.' Unless, of course, you are an Egyptian Pharaoh; and even then, being buried with it doesn't benefit anyone still living. Well, not for hundreds of years; and even then they get put in a museum for all the public to gawk at.

That's not to say that you shouldn't make sure that your descendants and family are taken care of. Keep in mind that if you spoil them with riches from a young age, they will not turn out having your integrity, chances are they will grow up to be ungrateful for everything in life. If you instil in them selfless generosity, you will give them something more valuable than thousands of your fortunes.

So, draw inspiration from the simple fact that there are so, so, so many financially richer people out there who are less intelligent than you. How do I know for sure? I meet them all the time. I also see them on television constantly. Chances are; they are also much poorer spiritually and emotionally than you. The point is, do not be jealous or resentful of those more affluent than yourself, only focus on improving your own financial situation. Then, when you reach their level financially you won't have anything to be jealous of.

Poverty

One day a father of a very wealthy family took his son on a trip to the country with the firm purpose of showing his son how poor people live.

They spent a couple of days and nights on the farm of what would be considered a very poor family.

On their return from their trip, the father asked his son, "How was the trip?"

"It was great, Dad."

"Did you see how poor people live?" the father asked.

"Oh yeah," said the son.

"So tell me, what did you learn from the trip?" asked the father.

The son answered: "I saw that we have one dog and they had four. We have a pool that reaches to the middle of our garden and they have a creek that has no end. We have imported lanterns in our garden and they have the stars at night. Our patio reaches to the front yard and they have the whole horizon. We have a small piece of land to live on and they have fields that go beyond our sight. We have servants who serve us, but they serve others. We buy our food, but they grow theirs. We have walls around our property to protect us, they have friends to protect them."

The boy's father was speechless.

Then his son added, "Thanks, Dad, for showing me how poor we are."

- Buddhist story I found on the internet

I changed my mind set, how do I start making money?

That's literally the million dollar question. So let's say you've been hacking your brain for several weeks straight and you're ready to take some inspired action. You may be asking how you can bring more in, if your income is capped at your JOB (Just Over Broke). Well, almost invariably you're going to have to make some business ventures on the side. What's a good business for you start playing with? Only your own subconscious mind can answer that, and it will do so in the form of an idea just shooting into your brain, attached with a sense of feeling good and certainty.

Ask questions to your subconscious like:

- 'What would I enjoy doing?'
- 'What can I do that seems fun and easy to me and will bring in money?' (Remember if it's too difficult, it's probably not the right way to go about it, it should be FUN!)
- 'What has my passion always been in, that I just forgot because the world, current job, and responsibilities took over?'

Chances are, if you're passionate about it, and find it fun; you will find a way to turn your passion into a business. Those tend to be the most fulfilling and profitable as well. Once you decide the area in which to develop a business, attack it from all angles to maximize your chances of success.

Firstly, research the commonalities in the ways of thinking of all wealthy people. There are many books on this subject; the 'Rich Dad Poor Dad' (by Robert Kiyosaki) books are excellent in my opinion.

Once your mind is functioning in line with creating a successful, money-making venture, it is time to start doing the practical research. Research similar businesses in the area and ascertain whether or not you can secure a piece of the pie, and more importantly whether the piece of pie will be worth it.

The money attraction experiment

This uses the Mind hacking experiment from Section 2, so get acquainted with that before you attempt this one.

First off, plug in a short-term monetary goal into the Mind hacking experiment. For example: 1,000 dollars of unexpected extra income at the end of this month.

Do the experiment for the next two weeks.

At the same time, be the most generous with your money for the next two weeks that you can be. For the next two weeks you want to give the message to the universe and your subconscious that you have more than enough. Try to feel really good while doing it too, this is very important. For example:

- Give that homeless person a dollar, or even five. (Don't think about the fact that they're probably going to use it for booze or drugs.)
- Donate some money to charity, or considerably more than usual if you already do.
- Buy your loved ones some 'no occasion' presents, and your partner a random 'just cause I love you' present.
- Anonymously deposit a bit of money into one of your poorest friend's accounts.

The point of living like this for the two weeks is to recondition your thought process to focus more on the joy of giving and sharing. The point is for your conscious mind to be happy with giving away money and not dwelling on 'not bringing in enough', all the while your subconscious is unobstructed and is conspiring with the universe to bring you even more money that you can spread joy with.

Again, after the two weeks you should stop the subconscious stuff for this goal and forget all about it. You can even stop the conscious effort of generosity; however after two weeks of getting all the joy from giving you may become addicted to the feeling.

Upon the completion of a successful experiment, you can expand your timescale and your requested amount.

Tithing

This is the easiest way to create a vibration wave that is on the frequencies of abundance. To signal to the universe that you are so thankful for your monetary abundance that you simply have to overflow and give some to others is definitely conducive to being financially wealthy.

How much should you give? Well the magic number floating about everywhere seems to be 10%. I personally believe that this number works particularly well due to some actual magic around the number 10. I think it amplifies the 'cosmic attraction power' through the Sacred Geometry of the number. Whether or not this is actually the case is probably irrelevant. All I know is that my money always seems to multiply around times when I've instantly given away 10% of a cheque I earned.

To whom should you give this money? Any positive cause is a noble one. You should give to a cause that's close to your heart to amplify emotional intensity of the gift.

Remember, whether it is something tangible or not, whatever you give away will return to you many fold.

Don't put all of your eggs in one basket, put them in several

Suppose you make a big lump sum of money. Would you suppose that your normal bank account is the best place for it? Obviously not! So how would divide up the funds? I suggest having at least a couple of different places to keep it all. For example, I have three bank accounts; two 'current' (normal) bank accounts and one savings one.

I use my main current account for all my day-to-day transactions like food, property (council) tax, booze, drugs, etc. (yes, in that order). Since in today's day and age card cloning and identity theft is rife, I suggest only keeping a few months of expenses here. Simply because if you're hacked, you won't lose it all; not that you'll 'lose it' but you won't feel the bite while you fill in insurance claim and fraud confirmation forms.

I use my second current account for short term goals. I don't make withdrawals from this account unless I have planned the purchase in advance. This one also acts as an emergency account, if in the off chance, my primary account is hacked.

I use my savings account for long term goals. When money is regularly deposited into this account, or if I pay in a lump sum (if it's been a specifically good month), I consider the money 'locked-in' and I only EVER use the money for the long term goal for which it was intended. This should always be the account in which I have the most money (excluding stocks/ bonds/mutual funds/etc.), simply because it tends to be the safest (access to this type of account is very limited, especially if you get only a basic cash card and no internet access) and least convenient way to get at your money. This could be a good thing, especially if you know you'll have to at least go to your bank to spend most of your money on some frivolous thing like a house or car. Not to mention they pay higher interest than normal bank accounts.

There are several reasons why I advocate physically separating your main pool of funds into several places. Firstly, it makes it so you can't spend your money on stupid crap when it's not in your most convenient (main) account. At least it makes it harder to. I only carry around my main account card (and an emergency credit card, in case my main card is cancelled by the clever bank people if some miserable criminal has cloned my card) in my wallet, and leave the other bank cards in a safe place.

Obviously, this is just what I do, and may not work for you. So feel free to make your own spin-off money management system that works for you. All I'm really trying to convey here is that keeping it all in a sock under your mattress is definitely not the way to go.

Make room in your life for it and prepare for the inevitable complications

For anything to effortlessly slip into your life, you should get your life ready and make room for its arrival. This applies a lot to money. Have all the houses you're going to buy planned out. Have a look at vacations you're going to take as soon as you're rich. Make it so that the money will be a perfect fit into your existence when it gets here.

As with anything you bring into your life, there may be complications. With money, there most certainly will be. Most of it will be in the form of resentments among your peers. The people you know that may not be financially blessed will be jealous. It is inevitable. Your job is to accept that this will be part of the process. You do however have options to make it as smooth as possible, with all your envious peers you can:

- Open their eyes to the ways of shifting their thinking about money
- Give them good jobs in your business
- With your capital, help them create a self-sufficient business
- When all else fails, you can just buy them a house or car, keeps the shallow friends happy and their resentment of you quite low ☺
- Replace or expand your peer group (Sounds cruel again, I know, but if they can't feel happy for you eventually, then why have them around?)

So get ready for the 'being rich will make you unhappy' and 'oh you think you're so much better with your big house and fancy suits' lines. Come to terms with the fact that your financial success will cause some resistance, and come up with your own pre-emptive plans for individuals you foresee being most problematic. Open your life to more money than you'll ever need flowing to you from infinite sources.

Prepare a room in your house for the money. Make its bed ahead of time. Cook it a meal and make a 'Welcome' banner for the front door. Then just anxiously know it's going to be coming home really soon. Do all of this metaphorically of course. ☺

Remember that financial abundance is your decision to make, not a fleeting hope that may or may not happen. So make the choice, and live truly free to go anywhere and do anything you want! It's not true freedom, but it's the closest you can currently have; with all the tyrannical, global government types and all.

Once you attain financial independence, don't forget that it's NOT the actual point of life. It is only a facilitator which opens a lot of doors to you, so that you can be free to pursue whatever avenues of fulfilment you deem suitable.

'What should I do after I'm rich', you ask?

Well, let's explore the notions of purpose and destiny in the following section.

Remember to *Attack your finances on all Fronts!*

Section 7 – Fate, Destiny and Purpose

If your Destiny is predetermined, what's the point of doing anything?

I've asked myself this question many times over the years, usually when confronted with religious people that believe that our fates are predetermined. However, when confronted with the obvious question, they don't really have an answer. What is the point of trying to accomplish something or change something when the future is already written in stone and any attempt will be futile? You might as well just accept everything life throws at you, because hey, it's predetermined.

Or maybe you were *meant* to try to change something which would get you to a different end result than the one you thought you were **meant** for, invariably arriving at the end result you were truly meant for.

Here is an interpretation that works especially well for me:

1) Fate exists – regardless of the specifics, we always arrive at what we subconsciously believe we are meant for
2) We constantly determine our own Fate – the more we concentrate and believe what our destiny on this earth is, the more it becomes true and the more we move towards it; we **can** and **do** change what we're meant for constantly, whether consciously or not

If we assume the preceding to be true, then the implications of this in our lives would be immense. Simply, destiny is an unstoppable force and we have the power to steer that force in any direction we choose. I believe we have ultimate power over our lives, inherently. It is just our 'conditioning' world that makes us forget our God-given power.

Most of us let all of our life choices be made for us, it's much easier. Once we make the decision that from now we will now take full responsibility for the results in our lives, we will become truly liberated.

Make your life whatever you want it to be, don't let anyone do your thinking for you.

Is choice an illusion?

I don't know, you choose. (Or do you?)
I personally believe that we actually do choose what we think but not what we do. Let me try to explain that one a bit. If we are free from external stimuli (i.e. an external thing isn't causing us to think about it) then we are free to wander with our thoughts anywhere we like.

We choose where we want to go in life. If we let this process be too passive, we will then choose the defaults according to our current subconscious way of thinking. The problem with being too passive in our decision making is that all the external influences that we are constantly flooded with start to direct our lives. If we take control however, we can choose to hold our own, chosen thoughts for longer and with much more intensity than others.

Now that we have chosen our current destiny with our thoughts, our physical behaviours will naturally flow into alignment with this destiny. For example, if we managed to program both our minds that we will definitely win in some contest (game show, sport, sweepstakes, lottery, etc.), then your subconscious will FORCE your conscious mind make all the right physical choices for that to occur. What we end up seeing is ourselves making conscious choices and winning as a result. Not to mention the Cosmos rearranging the 'mind-stuff' into the exact patterns for our desired result.

All we have to do is choose what to think about mostly and with most intensity, and trust that our actions will automatically align themselves to those thoughts. When we *consciously* choose with certainty, we *subconsciously* steer towards what we've chosen.

Once you believe you can freely choose **anything** at all you want for your life, what should you choose?

Your Meaning of Life

What is the meaning of all life? I don't think there is a single one; I think it changes from living being to living being. The meaning of life to a soldier ant is probably 'to serve the good of the colony'. As humans, we have a lot more diversity. Your purpose can be as general or specific as you want. You can say something like, 'I am here to provide the best service to people possible' or, 'I am here to help others'. Low-vibration people don't even take the time to explore such a thing as what is their self-imposed purpose. They simply give in to the notion that we are all just instinct-controlled animals. An aspect of MY purpose is to make sure YOU are not one of them.

Go ahead, find some paper and write down your *current* meaning of your life. Seriously, don't just think about it, write it down and put it somewhere where it can be readily read to remind you whenever you need it. It can be as long or short, specific or generic, greedy or selfless, ambitious or 'realistic' as you want.

> *"Ultimately, man should not ask what the meaning of his life is, but rather he must recognize that it is he who is asked."*
>
> Viktor E. Frankl

An important thing to note is that your life purpose is *dynamic*. At any point in your life, you can decide to have a new one or just refine your current one. Like you, your 'meaning of life' changes all the time. You should only consciously decide to change your current one when you're either bored of it or you notice your recent actions/thoughts/feelings pulling you in another direction.

So, search your heart for what you would love most to be the reason why you're here, then define it clearly and impose it on yourself. It could help to get in a slightly inebriated state if you're struggling; just to help bring down your mental barriers and inhibitions.

Relevance of physical actions

How important are all the behavioural choices we make? What colour of tie you decide to wear today, probably will not impact on whether or not you will close that big business deal. Or will it?

We must not put so much emphasis on details, when we have already chosen the end result. If you choose to get this particular job, for example, ahead of time, then all the seemingly conscious choices you make leading up to the interview have already been made for you. Did you ever notice that when you firmly decided you were going to get/achieve something, that you seemed to make all the right conscious choices and did, in fact, attain what you were after?

It wasn't luck; it was your conscious decision (choice of thoughts to eliminate the possibility of any other outcome) which triggered your subconscious into action to make all the right choices for you. Let's put this into perspective with a story that may or may not have happened. You should know by now that whether or not something is fiction or true doesn't really matter;

what matters is the message and concepts it's trying to convey. How many truths and **real** lessons did you learn from so-called 'imaginary' characters?

The instillation of 'Who I am' experiment

For the next two weeks, try this simple experiment and see how you feel about where your life is headed afterwards.

Get a clean sheet of paper that you'll be able to stick somewhere around the house where you visit every morning. Possibilities could be:

- Next to the bathroom mirror
- On the ceiling over your bed, or the wall next to your bed
- On the fridge, or beside the microwave
- On your front door

Now, on this page you are going to write a statement about who you are. It will be written only in the positive and only in the present. Whether it's all currently true or not is irrelevant, write what you aspire to be now. Make it only a couple concise sentences. Try to keep it hand-written in big letters, taking up most of the page.

For example:

I am John Smith, the most amazing blacksmith in the world! I have the most successful iron forge in the whole kingdom. I help all my villagers with my abundant wealth and am loved by everyone. I help to protect the world, one helmet and shield at a time.

Now that you have this aspiration statement stuck up at the location, simply read it once in the morning after waking, and once at night right before bed.

This will set up your subconscious mind for the whole day, and for your slumber. Soon all your levels of body, mind and soul will start believing it. Do this for a minimum of two weeks to see if you notice a change in your behaviours/quality of life. I personally do this every day, while making a new and updated statement every several months.

Also, you don't have to simply read it. You can sing it, yell it, close your eyes and chant it several times, or whatever else you feel like doing to ingrain it.

The naïve and the sceptical

Which of these extremes is better? Is it better to believe everything, or nothing and nobody at all? Most people will agree that you must be more of one of the other according to the particular situation. Let's explore what might happen if a married couple were to be comprised of these two extremes.

Once upon a time, there was a man and a woman who were on the opposite ends of this spectrum.

Zed considered himself to be a logical person. He was very dubious of anything and everything that deviated even slightly from his outlook on life. One could say he was a bit of a sceptic in all aspects.

Kristina was more emotional and superstitious. They were happily married and these differences actually made them complement each other. She was quite naive and believed in most things that sounded good, even if they were blatantly too good to be true.

One day, Kristina and her sister were out on the town shopping for shoes and handbags. They noticed an old-style Gypsy caravan where there usually was a fruit stall. A big sign read: KNOW YOUR FUTURE, OR CONTINUE BLIND. Under the words was a picture of some sort of hand with an eye at the centre. 'Hey, look! Let's get our fortune told', Kristina's sister said. She obviously agreed since she was superstitious and liked all that 'magical mumbo jumbo'.

Kristina's sister went in first. She came out a bit distressed and explained that the fortune-teller told her that she suffered in her marriage and would have to endure a couple more years before finally divorcing.

This made Kristina a bit apprehensive, but she went in anyway.

The fortune teller started the reading by looking at her hand and chanting some weird verses. Then she started laying down the Tarot cards. Kristina looked anxiously as the cards were turned face-up on the table. "This is a very fortunate card", the Gypsy said with much enthusiasm. She then proceeded to tell Kristina that she will get a huge sum of money in one month's time. Somewhere around 100,000 dollars in around 30 days, she then specified.

Needless to say Kristina came out ecstatic, cheering and celebrating to her sister, who could not share her happiness. When she came home, she quickly told Zed all about it. He did not share her optimism, as he was stuck in his logical cycle of earn, spend, survive. He told his wife, that there was no way that amount of money could just come to her out of the sky in that amount of time. Disregarding his pessimism, Kristina started celebrating everyday that her money was on its way.

About two weeks later Kristina received an email. It stated that the relative of a wealthy businessman was to inherit 5 million dollars; however they needed a bank account in Kristina's country to transfer the money to. If she would just send him the account details, she could keep 10% of it. She happily jumped up and down and told Zed about this amazing event. Zed quickly stated to her that it was a scam and she was not to respond to it at all. She insisted that THIS was the event that got her the money. Zed quickly pointed out that 10% of 5 million is 500,000 not 100,000. Kristina said she didn't care and was going to trust the mystery email. Luckily, Zed interjected and deleted the email before she had a chance to respond with the account details.

Kristina was furious; she didn't speak to Zed for the following two weeks. After forgetting all about her 'fortune', she does her usual shopping trip. The next day she checks her usual lottery numbers, and to her surprise she got 5 numbers and the bonus. She wins 104,000 dollars, 31 days after she had her fortune told.

Thanks to her blind faith, her belief made the money manifest. Thanks to Zed's scepticism she avoided getting scammed and having her bank account cleaned out. Both were needed to achieve the optimum result.

The moral of the story is that you should find your own happy balance between the two extremes. If you remember an event in your past where you were maybe taken advantage of because of your naivety, then obviously be more sceptical of similar situations in the future. Conversely, you may remember something that you missed out on because of your scepticism. Feel free to take a leap of faith next time a similar situation occurs.

Whether the fortune teller had a true clairvoyant gift is irrelevant, it was Kristina's belief in that fortune which made it come true.

Seriously? What's next, eye of newt in a cauldron?

No, I will not turn this section into a debate on whether or not there is any validity in what we conventionally deem 'Magic'. I personally believe that there are people with certain mental gifts (or curses depending how you look on them) who are able to see certain things that most of us cannot. I think we're ALL capable of seeing them, if we just knew how to unlock that potential.

I occasionally have 'psychic' dreams in which I'm in a setting I don't recognize, surrounded by people I don't know. Several months later, I find myself in that same situation, but by then I know where it is and the people around me. Weird eh?

Let us get back to clairvoyants though. First off, there are a lot of fakes out there who are just out to make a quick buck. However, the people with the true gift can actually see your future. Not your *set-in-stone*, absolute future, but the future that your current subconscious is heading towards.

You see, if you trust and believe that someone can TELL you your fortune, you are actually giving them the power to make up your future for you. Since you believe to your core their prediction, your subconscious will actually manifest it for you whether you fear it or embrace it strongly. This means that the frauds out there actually have the power to determine your future for you based on whether or not they like the look of you and/or if you tipped them well.

The few with the actual gift of foresight actually can see your future events but only based on your current way of 'vibrating'. If you believe someone is truly gifted in this way, try coming back for another 'reading' a week or so later and be in a completely different frame of mind and emotion. I can assure you that you will get a different reading, and even your 'real psychic' will be astonished.

I do believe that they are more in tune with the infinite consciousness and can simply see, in their minds, your future events based on your current subconscious vibration. I believe that fate can exist, and CAN be changeable. All they can see is further down the path along which you're currently going; you can always change your life path if you don't like the look of what's at the end.

Whatever someone told you or you told yourself you're destined for, it's never too late to change! Remember that your path in life is dynamic, you can (and do) change your direction at any time. Go any direction you want, anytime you want.

My Purpose

At this point you may be considering many options about what you think your current purpose of life should be. Let me give you the most specific example that I can expertly discuss: My own.

My personal current life purpose is *to spread Love and enlightenment throughout the world while developing all aspects of myself so that I can effectively help others.*

Sounds a bit hippie-ish, I know, but it is currently where I'm at.

When my youth becomes a distant memory, and I have 'achieved' all the major milestones of personal development that I currently have set out for myself, I aspire to have a life purpose along the lines of the following:

"May I become at all times, both now and forever

A protector for those without protection

A guide for those have lost their way

A ship for those with oceans to cross

A bridge for those with rivers to cross

A sanctuary for those in danger

A lamp for those without light

A place of refuge for those who lack shelter

And a servant to all in need."

His Holiness, the Fourteenth Dalai Lama
November 6, 2000

Until then, however, I have to focus on making myself wise, strong, Loving, compassionate, enlightened, resourceful and powerful enough to be able to help all those who need it. For now, I will still try to help everyone along the way; but in today's unfortunate world, you have to give a huge amount of time and energy on your own protection and growth before you can hope to help others.

Attack your meaning of life on all Fronts!

Section 8 – My Relevations

The time of civilized savagery

We all know that things only change in our lives when they MUST change. As Tony puts it, we make the biggest changes 'out of inspiration or desperation'. This also applies to our world as a whole. I recently went to a seminar where I was asked to think about anything that I wasn't confident about. I only came back with one answer: 'The future of the planet/human species'. I realized that I was totally confident in everything about ME, but had very little faith in how we as a human society were going to progress.

Let's go back for a minute to the times of our early-human ancestors. Violence and Dominance were the main tools of achieving anything you wanted. If I was cold, and wanted to sleep in a cave, I had to become a hunter/gatherer for the tribe, or I had to kill the Alpha Male and take his place as the dominant figure of the tribe. We've 'evolved' a lot since then as a species, but only in a superficial way. Let me explain that a bit. We have awesome technology, and our language and customs have come along greatly. So why is it that we're still faced with the same old 'human' problems? Why is there still so much ignorance and hate in the world? I think it's because we've let certain evils creep into our lives without even realizing that they're evil or that we practice them. Things like indifference, complacency, greed (not to be confused with healthy ambition, ☺), and FEAR. (Not the kind that keeps you alive, but the kind that stops you from helping yourself, others and stops humanity from making the world a better place)

"The greatest trick the devil ever pulled, was convincing the world he didn't exist"

- Charles Baudelaire

Throughout all of history, it is clear that one must contribute something of value to the cave, tribe, village, town, city, metropolitan, and now: The World; in order to receive anything of value in return. So it makes complete sense that we should keep on giving in order to receive. Stinginess, doing things half-assed, and hoarding our emotions and resources sets us up for not having any room in our lives for anything new and wonderful to enter into it.

Not to mention that those people always seem to have negative circumstances come into their lives, which will DRAIN their stockpile that they're so obsessed with hoarding. Do you personally know someone who worries about spending a penny and always complains about how tight money is, and tells you that YOU must save and save or YOU may not survive?

The world definitely needs a lot of help. There are more and more of these types of people all around. That doesn't mean however, that we are beyond all hope. There are still a lot of good people out there, although they're a bit of a rare breed. Let's make it our mission as a race to spread the message of Love to those of us who need it most; however, let's make sure we're strong enough to lift *them* up as to not let them bring *us* down.

"History will have to record that the greatest tragedy of this period of social transition was not the strident clamor of the bad people, but the appalling silence of the good people."

- Martin Luther King Jr.

Since then, I have realized that if I only touch a handful of people (not in that way, you pervert), and they, in turn, touch a handful of people each, the geometric scale in which enlightenment will spread throughout the world will be phenomenal!

And even more good news is that the spread has already started a while back, so the process has already started. Oh crap! I just realized that even by typing these words, I may be indirectly contributing to the spread of enlightenment. Good work, me.

Even YOU reading these words, and letting them take seed in your subconscious (even though you may be consciously saying, 'this stoner's lost his marbles') and moving at least a step closer towards ultimate enlightenment are part of the process.

And just with that, I had a tremendous revelation and have renewed my faith in mankind. Good work, infinite consciousness!

Keep in mind most of this book is written as the ideas are flowing from 'somewhere out there', through my mind, along my nervous system, straight into my fast-typing fingers. I must confess that almost half this book was written through my connection with the infinite; with the other half being actually consciously thought-out and analysed. Not to worry though, all the scientific studies and facts I referred to are well documented (somewhere out there), so go and do some research about them yourself!

Quasi-Structured ramblings on the world

What the hell have we done to the planet? Seriously, how badly are we treating the planet and each other? It is disgusting to see how huge evil corporations are treating us consumers, how governments can treat their citizens, how parents can treat their children and how we treat our kin and ourselves.

I could go on to give you depressing statistics about the global state of politics, economies, health, war, death, etc., but it would just perpetuate the energies that sustain these problems. Spreading awareness of a particular type of suffering only perpetuates it, I firmly believe this.

If people all around the world simply tried to live up to their own individual potentials and stopped worrying about all these 'problems' that they keep getting stressed about, I think we would finally have peace on Earth.

I think we are simply an immature species, not yet knowing our own limitless powers. All the horrible things in this world are simply symptoms of the 'frightened ego' trying cling on to this fleeting existence.

The key is to experience, enhance and truly live this physical existence and not try to simply prolong and perpetuate it.

It is all part of the bigger picture: Consciousness evolving to the next scalar level. We are the most integral part of the process, as we are the observers and the creators.

The world needs a good L.I.C.

"Slurp!" You may be thinking, as you picture a giant tongue rubbing against the planet. Not a 'lick', a L.I.C.

L = Love

I = Intellect

C = Courage

Capitalism could work perfectly, as could communism, if only the individual developed these three traits to the best of their abilities.

In my opinion, too many people never bother developing all three. For example there are lots of people who are very loving and smart, but lack the balls to convey it and back it up when it matters. Conversely, a street thug has lots of courage (takes some gall to try to rob/mug people), but absolutely lacks the love and intellect (or even common sense in most cases).

Then you have those lovely bimbos, the ones with all the love and courage (seem to have no fear of anything relevant and genuinely threatening, but will scream and run away from a shadow puppet) but not really anything between their ears. God bless those airheads! I sometimes wish I was born like that, because ignorance is bliss. However, because like me, you're probably not one of them, then we must seek the alternative road to bliss: Enlightenment.

And I strongly feel, that the way to enlightenment lies, at least partially, in the development of these three traits. I believe the trick is to stay balanced between the three, as this will unlock a tremendous amount of potential.

If everyone was fully loving, intelligent and brave we'd be living in Utopia. At the very least, the symptoms of this egotistical lifestyle would become a thing of the past.

Let's now examine a little story about what could happen when all these three traits are all greatly developed in an individual.

Gaia II

Aeons ago, the civilization of Atlantis was facing extinction. The world's water levels were going up, and they realized that pretty soon their entire great kingdom would be under water. Because of their advanced technology and understanding of the universe, they were able to create a portal (worm-hole) to another 'habitable' planet.

It then became clear to the elders of Atlantis, that the water level of the oceans and all the other natural disasters that have been occurring lately have all been self-defence mechanisms of Gaia (The spirit of the earth). It was clear that the evils of men were corrupting Gaia past the point of comfort. So, just like any living organism, she's trying to purge the disease. It is important to note, that as a species, we are inherently symbiotic with our planet's spirit. We are meant to live in harmony with the Earth and each other.

When enough damage is done that it actually affects the pure spirit that resides within our planet, the planet has no choice but to defend itself.

Even though they were the most enlightened people at the time, there was still a great debate within Atlantis as to how to proceed. About half of Atlantis' citizens wanted to use the worm hole and leave the planet for the still-pure planet they dubbed Gaia II.

The other half argued that it was their responsibility to save Earth; obviously with the opposite assumption that, in fact, it COULD be saved.

So it was that the great civilization of Atlantis was split in two. The city and half the citizens used the worm hole and started a new colony on Gaia II. The other half remained here and dispersed throughout the lands; they knew their task was going to be long and arduous.

So they started to integrate themselves into global society and breeding with the locals. They passed on their wisdom and compassion down through the generations with their teachings and their DNA. Nearly every major technological discovery, every medical breakthrough, every positive government change and every masterpiece of art came from a member of the Atlantian bloodline.

They are still among us; making scientific advancements, enhancing our society, understanding us, and most importantly, loving us. Let's show them all that their sacrifice was not in vain. Let's live the most loving lives we can, we'll show them that we are worth saving.

Doomsday in 2012

Most people have heard about the Mayan prophecy of December 21, 2012. If you're haven't, let me bring you up to speed. Basically the world as we know it will end. The ancient tribe of Maya has a calendar which is basically more accurate than our own. This calendar ends on that date. We are basically now in what they refer to as the 'End Time'. Sometime around the date, some dramatic cataclysms will occur and will change our world forever.

After loads of research, to everyone in the world, I can honestly say 'Do Not Be Afraid'!

If you don't believe the prophecy, then obviously you have nothing to worry about in the first place.

If you DO believe in the prophecy, you also have no reason to worry. If you research it deeper, you will find out that humanity will survive according to the prophecy. The systems that we currently have on earth won't. The money, the wars, the evils of this current world will cease to exist. This will be the civilization's evolutionary leap. Simply do not fear the change. It should be something to look forward to, not fear. Our civilization will finally reach the ultimate level of consciousness.

What do I personally believe will actually happen? Since I have no control over whether or not this happens, I'm not going to focus time and energy towards it until closer to the date. When that date does start approaching though, I'm going to make sure my heart is true, my thoughts are positive, and my fallout shelter is well-stocked. Well I don't want to be taken out by a falling tree or flying cow when the hurricanes start blowing.

This could be concurrently looked at from the scientific angle. I believe that the 'destroyer' who is going to catalyse all these planetary changes is that elusive 'Planet X'. (AKA *Nibiru*: Believed to be a Brown Dwarf [kind of like a sun, but too low in mass to sustain stable hydrogen fusion] which is believed to be coming closer to our Solar system) The Mayans must have found a way to calculate Planet X's orbit around our sun and made the calendar according to this.

There are scientists that believe a Polar Shift and other environmental anomalies will be caused by Planet X being at its closest point to our sun.

This will cause solar winds and storms that will have a huge impact on the Earth.

Even the scientists say that this will pass within a couple of months. See, even the worst case scenario isn't that bad if you're prepared. Play some video games and maybe get shoot some footage of what you see in the sky for all those weeks of transition.

The way I see it, something HAS to happen soon. What exactly, I do not know. I do know that the Spirit of this planet (Gaia) is either going to try to pacify and enlighten us, or shake us off. Perhaps it will be both at once? Take comfort in the fact that everything will turn out alright after this period.

Do your own research about Mayan 2012 prophecies if it interests you, but be warned; it may make you go crazy for an extended period of time.

The final battle for our world and our souls: Hippies vs. Fat Cats

There is a revolution that is slowly rising up around the world.

The ones rising up: the new age, enlightened people that believe in Love, Gratitude, Tolerance, Wisdom and that have faith that the Evils of this world will one day dissolve and the human race will finally be free and enlightened. Although this is not completely accurate, let's call them (us) Hippies for short.

The ones currently in control and will do anything to quell the rebellion: the 'Unlightened', Greedy, Power-Hungry, Fear-Mongering assholes that are never truly happy, but live from moment to moment surviving on the satisfaction that someone is less fortunate or they were able to control someone. Let's call them Fat cats for short.

The crux of the matter is that Hippies cannot convert Fat Cats to the enlightened ways of thinking forcefully; they can only live by example.

I believe there is a happy balance that can be reached. Hippies will eventually take decisive, positive action towards a brighter future, instead of just boycotting showers and smoking pot. Conversely, Fat Cats will realize the folly of their materialistically-obsessed perceptions and start acting ethically while discovering this abstraction called Love.

If the balance is not reached, then both sides will be destroyed and the world will be plunged into darkness. Remember the stages that all great discoveries go through.

All profound truth goes through these three phases:

[As examples, let's observe what an average person back in the 1500s might have said to Nicolas Copernicus]

1) **It is ridiculed**
   'Haha, shut up Copernicus! If the world is round, then let's just all run quickly and make it turn faster! You idiot!'

2) **It is violently opposed**
   'Kill him! He's some sort of sorcerer!'
   'Do you repent your Heresy?'
   'Even God says that the world is flat'

3) **It is accepted as self evident**
   'Of course the world is round, what kind of idiot would think otherwise'
   [Probably said by the same guy who just several years back called to lock up N.C. for heresy]

No different is the fate of the universal truths I tried to convey in the preceding pages.

Final Thoughts

It won't hurt to try it, I promise

Although you may not accept or see personal value in some of the strategies and methods I've discusses in these pages, would it really hurt to try them? What's the worst that could happen?

Worst Case: You are richer for the experiences of trying to make some sort of improvement in a particular area of your life. You get some great short-term results, but then your negative beliefs take over and drag you back down to your subconsciously-comfortable level. In the long term you are only 5% better in each area of life. Yes, this is the worst case scenario if you've read this whole book and tried to fully understand each section.

Best Case: You could actually initiate some sort of improvement or progress in a particular area of your life. You could feel inspired to share that particular distinction/idea/strategy with someone close, who in turn implements it and also gets a positive result. After helping many people achieve some positive result, you feel so inspired that you get another idea that derives from a tangent to something I've written, and you help even more people with it. Because of your inspiration now, you become a world-renowned visionary and are consulted for advice on the particular topic by high-profile people from around the world! Hey, it could happen...

Most likely, if you try anything that I've suggested in this book, your result will be somewhere between the two.

Some key points to take with you

- Make **Love** your #1 priority
- Do try some if not all the suggestions and experiments in this book
- Don't let anyone stress you out
- Believe completely in the infinite power of your own heart and mind
- Accept the fact that your physical reality is relative to your perception
- Be generous with your emotions, thoughts, money and other resources

- Try not to be judgemental of others, even and especially if they've wronged you
- Keep in top mental and physical health so you have more to give of yourself
- Help someone whenever you can
- Never stop learning and expanding your awareness
- Attempt to eliminate rigidity and negativity in your life
- Surround yourself with beauty: sensory, emotional, mental and spiritual
- Create something of value to benefit humanity whenever you get a chance

Until our thoughts meet again

So we arrive now, at the end of this book. I have rather mixed feelings. I am so happy that I've kept you listening to my thoughts as you've progressed through this book, but a little saddened that I must now leave you. For you see, as I've been writing this book, I've held a picture of you reading it as if we were doing it both at the same time. Although some 'time' separates us, and I do not yet know exactly how, but I have felt a developing rapport with you.

I know you are full of potential, and I sincerely hope that with my words I have helped you to unlock a little bit more of it.

Just in case you happen to absolutely love this book, make sure to check out www.attacklifeonallfronts.com and www.anvomir.com for all my future titles

My words were intended for you, share them with whoever you feel will benefit from them. Love, Peace and Enlightenment be with you good reader; until our individual consciousnesses cross paths again, I bid you a fine farewell.

End Communication...

Lightning Source UK Ltd.
Milton Keynes UK
UKOW04f1246160615

253587UK00001B/5/P

9 781907 652103